INTERNSHIPS

Theory and Practice

Charles H. Sides, PhD
Ann Mrvica, EdD

Fitchburg State College, Massachusetts

Baywood's Technical Communications Series
Series Editor: CHARLES H. SIDES

Routledge
Taylor & Francis Group
LONDON AND NEW YORK

First published 2007 by Baywood Publishing Company, Inc.

Published 2017 by Routledge
2 Park Square, Milton Park, Abingdon, Oxon OX14 4RN
711 Third Avenue, New York, NY 10017, USA

Routledge is an imprint of the Taylor & Francis Group, an informa business

Library of Congress Catalog Number: 2006033245
ISBN 13: 978-0-89503-355-0 (hbk)

Library of Congress Cataloging-in-Publication Data

Sides, Charles H., 1952-

Internships : theory and practice / by Charles H. Sides and Ann Mrvica.
p. cm. -- (Baywood's technical communications series)
Includes bibliographical references and index.
ISBN-13: 978-0-89503-355-0 (cloth : alk. paper)
ISBN-10: 0-89503-355-0 (cloth : alk. paper) 1. Internship programs--United States. 2. College students--Employment--United States. 3. School-to-work transition--United States. 4. Career education--United States. I. Mrvica, Ann, 1955- II. Title.

LC1072.I58M78 2007
331.25'922--dc22

2006033245

Dedication

We dedicate this book to two of our former colleagues who have remained largely and unjustifiably unknown for what were truly revolutionary accomplishments in the mid-1970s: Lee DeNike, EdD and David Ryder, EdD, both professors emeriti in the Department of Communications Media at Fitchburg State College.

Dr. Ryder was instrumental in establishing the department in the mid-1970s, envisioning it as an academic department that would educate professionals for the newly emerging field of technology-based communications. His vision was firmly founded on the conceptual work of Vannevar Bush at the Massachusetts Institute of Technology and World Wide Web iconoclast Steve Nelson. Rendering the work of these visionaries practical enabled Dr. Ryder to create one of the more unique academic departments in the United States, a professional department that was soundly based in accepted communications theory and design principles, and also provided state-of-the-art, hands-on professional experience to its students from their freshman year through graduation. His first faculty appointment was Dr. Lee DeNike.

Prior to his retirement, Dr. DeNike established and directed the department's internship program for its first 23 years. He foresaw that a semester-long, full-time, unpaid professional internship would provide students with experience that could not be gained in any other pedagogical method. Even today, more than a quarter of a century after its creation, the internship program of the Department of Communications Media at Fitchburg State College remains one of the few in the country to require of its students an internship of this duration and rigor. Dr. DeNike's vision has been instrumental in securing an over 90% professional placement ratio for the hundreds of graduates who have successfully completed their academic program at the college.

Our contributions have been minimal by comparison.

Ann Mrvica, EdD
Charles H. Sides, PhD

Preface

For years, managers at companies and organizations with which we have had long-term internship relationships have suggested that a book be written which describes the full-time, semester-long, unpaid professional internship that functions as the capstone graduation requirement for the Department of Communications Media at Fitchburg State College. This book is a response to those requests.

We take no false pride that the program described here is the only or even the best approach to providing professional experience to college students; we do know, however, that it has been successful for our students since the mid-1970s—long before the current interest in outcomes assessment, portfolio assessment, and other *en vogue* pedagogies. We also know from over 25 years of experience that internship programs of this breadth and depth are relatively rare in colleges and universities. A similar approach might very well work for the readers of this book and their institutions of higher education, too.

It is our belief that internships, as conceived in this book, are not particularly new; rather, they are a pedagogy that society, especially postindustrial western society, is returning to, as knowledge professions evolve more and more into what employees can do (*techne*), as opposed to a fixed set of information possessed by those employees (*episteme*). The distinction between these Aristotelian concepts is one of the foundations of this book. Teaching students the importance of lifelong learning has become a watchword at colleges and universities. Internships are one way of instilling the value in that practice early on in a young professional's life. This is another of this book's themes.

In many ways, this book is a beginning. We hope to provide a historical and theoretical foundation for internships as a valuable part of the academic experience. We also hope to provide useful suggestions to college faculty and administrators seeking to design successful internship programs, as well as to corporate managers seeking to participate in the professional learning experiences that successful internship programs can provide. We realize, however, that this is an enormous task, and that one book-length work could never complete it. Accordingly, important work remains. Future research might inquire more deeply into the theoretical underpinnings of internships, particularly the roles of *techne*, *episteme*, *poiesis*, and *praxis* as they apply to learning and performance during internship experiences. Quantitative research might be designed that would provide cost-benefit comparisons between full-time and part-time internships, paid and unpaid internships, and internships that occur early in a students academic career versus those that occur at the end. Other ideas, we hope, will be stimulated by reading this book. In closing, we bring our experiences to this book, and with them we acknowledge our biases. It is our hope that readers will evaluate the experiences, look past the biases, and find much here that they can use.

Ann Mrvica, EdD
Charles H. Sides, PhD

Acknowledgments

In any endeavor such as this one, many people are due our gratitude. Our department colleague Rob Carr provided a thorough and extremely helpful review and edit of the working draft of this book. Much of what is valuable in the book is a result of his close reading and suggestions. He and other colleagues in our department—Gunther Hoos, Randy Howe, and Helen Simmons—have supervised sections of internships and shared their experiences with us. Other colleagues—Robert Harris, Jon Krasner, Peter Laytin, Charles Roberts, and Jeff Warmouth—donate valuable time every semester to preparing and qualifying students for their prospective internships. We also benefit from an extraordinary college administration that has supported this program from its inception, funded the supervision that is required for the program to be a success, provided release time for the person who directs and manages it, and consistently recognizes that a required, full-time, unpaid professional internship held in our students' senior year is one of the pillars of success for a large department in a small state college, which many people have never heard of.

Former students also willingly allowed us to include their work as examples of excellence in this book. Specifically, we thank Adam Moore for a sample of his internship journal, Nicole Slaven for her internship log summary, Courtney Parsons for a sample of her daily log, Nicole Cloutier for her professional statement, Benjamin Mabe for his portfolio sample, Julie Scholl for her final internship analysis paper, and Edson Andrade, Tim Kafalas, Tobias Goulet, and Andrea Bruno for their résumés. Each of these students are among hundreds who entered into their internships enthusiastically and professionally as the first step to their careers. Many of our corporate partners also contributed to this book. These include Amy O'Brien Jeyarajan at the North of Boston Convention and Visitors Bureau, Ellen Wallet at Arnold Worldwide, Jessica Holland at W. K. Bradford Publishing

Company, Dawn Haley at Fablevision, Susan Templeton at the North Central Massachusetts Chamber of Commerce, Harris Upham at PowPix Productions, and Anne-Marie Aigner at Aigner Associates. In addition, this book could not have been completed without the long and consistent partnership of our internship host sites throughout the United States, Canada, and Europe. While they are too many to name, the wisdom we have gained through years of working with them is incalculable.

Contents

CHAPTER 1
Introduction

School to work, learning by doing, work to learn, apprenticeships, internships. By whatever name we choose to call them, opportunities through which students experience their chosen professions before formally entering into them are in the process of becoming a staple of twenty-first-century education. Internships—the name by which these experiences will be called in this book—are supervised introductory career opportunities provided in partnership between academic institutions and professional organizations. They are not new, however. Their existence is traceable back through centuries of published work and suspected perhaps to the very dawn of humanity itself as each set of skills is passed on to the next generation by persons teaching others through demonstrated and jointly participated experiences.

In some ways, the immediate past century or so may have been an aberration—a time in which learning was inculcated more and more frequently through lecture and book than through experience. If so, then we are positioned to return to a long-proven, successful method of developing knowledge and skills in succeeding generations of professionals.

Aristotle was among the first to explore these important distinctions in ways of learning and being. According to him, *techne* is identical to "a state of capacity to make, involving a true course of reasoning. All art is concerned with coming into being, i.e., with contriving and considering how something may come into being which is capable of either being or not being, and whose origin is in the maker and not in the thing made" [1]. He differentiates *techne* from *episteme*, or theoretical knowledge. In other words, Aristotle's use and explanation of *techne* involve the arts and crafts of making things; *episteme* involves the knowledge about things, or what Aristotle would associate with science. In the *Nicomachean Ethics*, Aristotle envisions *techne* as a type of activity out of which is created a durable good, a product or state of affairs. This might include an architect designing and building a house, a potter making a goblet, or a physician restoring a person to health. This type of production, which Aristotle called *poiesis*, can be precisely specified by the maker before he or she engages in the activity. But Aristotle went beyond this concept to explore *praxis* as well, which he described as "conduct in a public space with others in which a person . . . acts in such a way as to realize excellences that he has come to appreciate in his community as constitutive of a worthwhile way of life" [2].

While it is far beyond the capacity and thesis of this book to explore these concepts in depth, it is our belief that internships, as a form of learning through experience, exhibit important aspects of *techne, poiesis,* and *praxis,* and that through these, knowledge communities are created and sustained throughout one's professional life. We also believe that these knowledge communities have long been one of the foundational principles of society, and that as knowledge industries become more important to global economies, these concepts will again, in the twenty-first century and beyond, manifest the importance Aristotle foresaw in them. These concepts will be explored more carefully in Chapter 2, Internships as Learning Experiences.

HISTORY OF INTERNSHIPS

Perhaps the earliest reference to internships occurs in Hammurabi's Code, in which the appropriateness of "bringing a boy into the home of a craftsman" is declared as the "natural way to learn a craft" [3, p. 63]. Similarly, early writings among Greek, Roman, Chinese, and Vedic communities suggest that the employment of internships in order to prepare youths for entry into various skilled fields was widespread and increasingly formalized among developing societies as early as 600 BCE. While Aristotle's exploration of *techne* in the *Nicomachean Ethics* does not specifically refer to the importance of internship in transmitting the knowledge of doing and making to succeeding generations, it is safe to assume that the practice was so common in Athenian society that it did not require acknowledgment.

Current approaches to internship trace their origins at least to the Middle Ages, during which such experiences were controlled by guilds, associations of craftsmen (and in some cases, women) who banded together to promote mutual interests shared by others engaged in their trades. In medieval times, apprentices were engaged for a period of years "while they were initiated into the theory and practice . . . associated with a particular occupation," which could include both manual and professional pursuits [4, p. 15]. In the twenty-first century, the professions of law and medicine continue to exhibit aspects of this approach to professional education.

When considering the history of internships, particularly as it concerns the practices of craft guilds and apprenticeship in the European Middle Ages, it is important to remember that society was evolving from the feudal manorial tradition to a burgeoning entrepreneurial, trade-based tradition with the concomitant rise of a middle class. Crafts, trades, and apprenticeships were ways in which serfs and other indentured peoples bought their freedom in the Middle Ages. Although the vast majority of these experiences were limited to men, the importance of this trend becomes increasingly evident when one considers the role of women at the time and how internships could become a means of empowerment and independence in what was largely, for women, a powerless and dependent society.

Women and Internships in the Middle Ages

A considerable collection of written records has survived from the High Middle Ages (thirteenth-sixteenth centuries) both in the form of pipe rolls from particular boroughs, which record persons taking out their freedom in the form of establishing a trade, and from court proceedings that record legal disputes between guild members or against them. While the overwhelming majority of these records mention only men, some establish the participation of women in the trades of the day. And in each of the cases discussed below, one can assume that the women learned their craft through apprenticeship, most likely serving either their fathers or husbands or some other male relative in order to gain the practical knowledge required to enter a profession; in rare examples, as will be seen, the master craftsman may have, in fact, been a woman who then, in turn, mentored other women's entry into the trade.

As representative of the development of trades, one can consider the York Register of Freemen, which runs continuously from 1273 through the early 1500s. In doing so, it is important to realize that male artisans rarely "set up shop" on their own; instead, it was far more common for a man to wait until he married in order to establish a production system that could include wife, children, and extended family. While the law of the day (*femme sole*) allowed women to trade in their own right, it was not regularly exercised, except in the case of surviving widows of craftsmen. Yet exceptional examples and even exceptions existed among a wide variety of trades: victuallers, textiles, leather, metals, building, and others.

Victuallers included bakers, brewers, butchers, fishmongers, graziers, hostelers, hucksters, and so forth. At this time, bakers made a variety of breads: white, brown, black, and horse. White bread (wastel, simnel, cocket, or domain) was the finest available and cost approximately one penny per loaf. Brown (bastard wastel or bastard simnel) cost a halfpenny per loaf. Black bread (*panis integer*) was coarse and cost only a farthing. Horse bread was made from the lowest qualities of flour and was generally considered not fit for human consumption. Because of the importance of bread as a staple in the Middle Ages, there were numerous regulations regarding its production and distribution. While few women are listed as master bakers in surviving rolls, it is suspected by tangential evidence, including the fact that most medieval craftsmen could not afford to set up practice until they had a wife and family, that much of the bread was baked by women.

The same is true of the brewing trade, which was responsible for the creation and selling of alcoholic beverages. The most common association to women in this trade comes in the term "alewife," which usually referred to a woman who was involved in the brewing trade and whose husband was often in a related trade—baker, for example, because of the related use of yeast. "Evidence shows that women made as much if not more of the ale and beer served in the Middle Ages as men" [5].

Women were at times found in the butcher trade as well, usually following the death of their husbands. Interestingly, legal records indicate a disproportionate amount of the fining of women for leaving dung and entrails in the street when compared with men in the same craft. Fishmongers, too, were at times women, and most readers are no doubt aware of this even subconsciously through the survival of such children's songs as "Molly Malone," in which the main character of the song was a seller of shellfish. Like numerous nursery rhymes and folk songs, this one almost certainly dates back at least to the Middle Ages.

The growing association of inns and victualler trades in the Middle Ages provided another opportunity for women. It was quite common for a master craftsmen to have a wife who ran an inn associated with his craft—either in the form of rooms in the main building or in a separate building altogether. The first recorded female innkeeper dates from 1526, though certainly they are suspected from times earlier than this, as court records indicate innkeepers of both genders being prosecuted for a variety of offenses prior to this date.

Textile industries provided an almost natural opportunity for women in the Middle Ages, growing out of their responsibilities for clothes making, which date back into prehistory. Women were tailors, even if the majority of them worked for a master male tailor and remained in obscurity. Some, however, did stand out in wills where they were identified by their trade. One example is Margaret de Knaresburgh, tailor, who in 1398 bequeathed two gold rings and six silver spoons in her will.

Weaving was performed almost entirely by women. Isabella Nonhouse, who purchased her freedom in 1441, two years after her husband's death, is listed in the York Register as a master weaver. Those women who bought their freedom in such ways began to band together to become entrepreneurs, forming groups of organized female laborers. In the leather trades it was similar, as cardmakers (craftpersons who set metal teeth into strips of leather used for carding wool) were most frequently referred to with feminine pronouns, even in instances where they were never identified.

Even in metal trades there are cases of women involved in the craft. Although one thinks of armorers as being exclusively male, there is at least one recorded instance of a woman engaged in this trade. Agnes Hecche of York was trained by her father as an armorer. More frequently, there are cases of women involved in the making of chain mail, since the drawing of wire was a less physically demanding task than the shaping of sheet metal.

Women are also listed as potters, owning and operating large, respectable foundries. Margaret Soureby in York and Joan Hille in London are two examples. In Paris, certain metal trades such as the manufacture of fine jewelry, were reserved specifically for women's guilds, in which women were apprenticed to women.

Building trades were not exempt from the contribution of women either. Katherine Rolf of Cambridge took time off from her customary occupations of spinning, candle making, and threshing for the nuns of St. Radegund's to help thatch the roof of the nunnery. There are also examples of women carpenters, shipwrights, plasterers, and plumbers [4]. And in all of these trades, of which the somewhat gritty history survives today, internship was the means by which new craftspeople, both men and women, were brought into the professions and into the guild systems that controlled them.

LEGAL CODIFICATION OF INTERNSHIPS

Internships, as they developed from the Middle Ages to the Renaissance, became a significant aspect of society, encompassing "social, occupational, educational, religious, familial, group, and legal dimensions. [They were] a central core [of experience] which impinged in a variety of ways upon individuals, males and females, young and old alike, and upon communities large and small" [6, p. 21]. Two acts of Parliament in Elizabethan England helped define the types of internship that had evolved by the late 1500s and early 1600s. The Statute of Artificers (1563) and the Poor Law Act (1601) suggest that essentially two genres of internship had emerged by mid-millennium. One was the classic system of internship inherited from medieval guilds and codified in the Statute of Artificers (sometimes called the Statute of Apprentices) of 1563. "On paper, this was the most comprehensive plan for the economic life of a country that any European government had made [to this point] . . ." [7, p. 229]. Conditions for these experiences were now specified in writing, as the statute's goal was to preserve existing class structures, locate and fixate industry, and regulate the transference of labor from one place or occupation to another. Despite the restrictiveness of this act in principle, its application was frequently more lenient. Local magistrates, responsible for the administration of the statute, frequently granted exceptions, with the result being an actual lessening of restraints upon trade, internship, labor contracts, and other aspects of professional life. The Poor Law of 1601 differed primarily in that it was an outgrowth of systems that had evolved over a half-century to deal with burgeoning numbers of poor in English society, as the medieval manorial system evolved into more modern forms of societal structure. As the poor left the manors, they gravitated to towns and cities, bringing with them concomitant problems of vagrancy, begging, and increases in crime. The Poor Law dealt with this in a variety of ways—from specifying punishments for different types of poverty to specifying obligations of parishes toward the poor to providing for the binding of children of the poor as apprentices in trades [8].

Internships in the New World

The United States' origin as a British colony has demonstrably affected historical approaches to internship here. In colonial America, internships were a staple of industrial education. Benjamin Franklin spent time as an apprentice in a printer's shop; many others, known and unknown, shared similar experiences in a variety of trades. In essence, the American approach to internship reflected British traditions modified to meet the particular needs and conditions that existed in the colonies. Town governments set the laws and conditions of internships. Officials had responsibility for managing the agreements between master and apprentice, and this approach lasted until well into the nineteenth century, in various trades [9].

However, eventually internship education failed in the United States for several reasons. One is that it "lacked organization, sufficient administration, supervision, and any related . . . classroom instruction" [9, p. 8]. Early American internships focused on manual skills and, as a result, could not meet the growing needs for technological knowledge and skills that were developing during the Industrial Revolution. What has become thought of as classical approaches to internships could not, therefore, provide requisite knowledge and thinking skills that were being increasingly required in modern industry. Another reason for the failure of internships in the United States has been attributed to the democratic ideology that is fundamental to American society. Schools, rather than internships, have been promoted as the guarantors of democracy [3, p. 67].

For internships to reemerge as a significant and successful form of professional education would require a rethinking of their purpose, design, and operation. To that end, it is helpful to understand the various stages and types of internship experience.

Models of Internship Experiences

Internships provide an opportunity for those engaged in them to "learn the process of self-generating skill, which involves learning how to undertake continuous learning. The master [of a craft, trade, or profession] is a continuous learner where the problems to be solved are generated by engagement with the trade through the application of skill and knowledge with an underlying confidence and attitude toward production and the product" [7, p. 62].

Using this perspective, three models of internship have developed over the centuries: classical, modern, and postmodern. Classical internships, such as those characterized and formalized by the medieval guild experiences, involve

- time serving. The intern is required to spend a predetermined period of time learning the trade or craft.
- training by observation and learning by doing. Masters in the trade or craft demonstrate skills to the intern and provide opportunities to learn by guiding them through planned experiences.
- experiences coupled with formal education. As internships evolved, formal education became more and more prevalent as a complementary experience. In modern times, this has led to the development of trade and vocational schools devoted specifically to practical and technical education.
- specialized training in a single trade. Interns learn a specific trade or occupation and focus their entire attention on that single occupation.
- inculcation of craft pride and craft mysteries. By learning an occupation from an expert, pride in the trade is passed along to the next generation of professionals.

Modern internships, such as those that exist in an increasing number of professions today, involve

- training to standards of craftsmanship. As internships evolved into modern times, standards were developed to determine entry requirements into an occupation.
- supervised training. Internship supervision has become more formalized and prescribed in many occupations.

- experience coupled with college study. Again, in many occupations, college study is required as a complement to and preparation for internship experiences.
- contracts of employment. Formalized contracts between internship host organizations, the intern, and educational institutions have become more common as a way of describing and prescribing the internship experience, formalizing what host institutions will provide, the intern's responsibilities, and the educational institution's expectations and requirements.
- emphases on attainment of formal qualifications, such as degrees and certifications, depending upon the profession. Once again, depending upon the occupation, internships may lead to a variety of formal proofs that the intern is ready to enter the profession.
- formalized entry into professions by means of tests, interviews, application forms, and stipulated qualifications. A variety of implements are employed to determine an intern's fitness for entry into an occupation.
- flexibility demonstrated by trade specialization combined with training in transferable areas and related disciplines. As more and more scholars point to the necessity of transferable skills and knowledge among professionals in a twenty-first-century society, internships and vocational or professional education have begun to provide opportunities for learning in related fields.
- results-oriented experiences and a focus on the importance of quality in the profession. Here, too, an emphasis on what has come to be called "outcomes assessment" stresses the importance of attaining measurable levels of quality in an intern's or professional's performance.

Postmodern internships, such as those that will be promoted in this book, involve

- training to specified standards. This remains similar to the modern internship.
- contract of employment. This, too, is a valuable matter retained from modern internships.
- formalized entry into professions by means of tests, interviews, application forms, and stipulated qualifications. Again, this is a holdover from modern internships.

- flexibility demonstrated increasingly by a focus on transferable skills needed in professions that are changing more quickly than ever. This important aspect of modern internships will become even more valuable in the ever-changing twenty-first-century professional environment.
- lifelong learning focus [10]. The most valuable professionals will be those who continue to learn and upgrade their knowledge and skills throughout their professional lives.

THE FUTURE: INTERNSHIPS AND NEW MODES OF LEARNING

Peter Senge's thesis in *The Fifth Discipline* is that successful twenty-first-century corporations will have to become what he calls "learning organizations" [11]. Peopled by lifelong learners, these organizations will quickly and constantly be in the process of reconceptualizing themselves in order to react productively and profitably to ever-changing markets. Sides' work in *Technical Communication Frontiers: Essays in Theory* points out the role of communities in professional environments and how those communities change through the interplay of discordance and consensus [12]. Drawing upon the work of Hegel, he suggests that within disciplines, communities exist and are constantly in the process of evolving in terms of their shared values and structure. The history of internships demonstrates the effects such community consensus has had on how internships are designed and applied.

For example, internships originated as successful and time-honored methods for passing along discrete skills from one generation of artisan to another. Within that milieu, a certain social structure evolved and was maintained, coming to full fruition in the medieval guild system. Artisans within the system understood their responsibilities, their needs, and their contributions to society. They developed what we would call today a mindset—a way of looking at and operating within their world. As society continued to evolve into the world of the Industrial Revolution, perceptions changed, as did responsibilities, needs, and the contributions individual workers made to society. And at the height (or depth, depending upon one's perception) of the Industrial Revolution's effect on the individual, mindset changed as well. It changed so much that society began to call into question the value systems of treating human individuals as cogs in the machine. As a result, perceptions changed again; mindset changed again. Union movements led to a reconsideration of the individual, his or her worth, needs, responsibilities, and contributions to society. The current mindset of the "knowledge work" evolved, and it looks much more like the artisan of antiquity, performing in a new conceptualization of craft. As such, internships as preparatory training and inculcation stand ready to once again take their rightful place in the education of present and future professionals.

Using such past studies as foundation, internships may be viewed through the works of such cultural anthropologists as Lave [13], Lave and Wenger [14], and Engestrom [15] as the basis for a social theory of learning.

Internships and Social Theories of Learning

As one attempts to foresee the future of internships, it becomes clear that the renewed interest in them results from a number of issues. Perhaps the most consistent is that a number of governments, particularly the United States and in Europe, are attempting "to strengthen the skill base of their future work force by establishing a new form of [internship] that fulfills some of the functions of traditional craft [internships], but takes into account their weaknesses and the new demands of [twenty-first-century economies]" [16]. Equally important is the work of Senge [11] and others who have predicted that if societies in the future are to be economically competitive, they have to become learning societies peopled with lifelong learners. Interestingly, however, it has been noted that in the literature proposing and examining learning organizations, learning societies, and lifelong learning, there has been little examination of the processes of learning itself [15].

Following the recent work of certain cultural anthropologists [16, 17], Guile and Young [18] have suggested that internships may form the basis for a social theory of learning. Existing theories of learning tend to focus on behaviorist and individualist assumptions; they tend to be dependent upon transmission pedagogies as well as the transfer of decontextualized knowledge to vocationally specific contexts. They are frequently associated with cognitive-science accounts of expertise as the stable individual mastery of well-defined tasks. Viewing internships as the basis for a "reflexive theory of learning" [19] permits them to be reconceptualized in ways more suitable to twenty-first-century environments.

Since the beginning of the Industrial Revolution, sociologists and political economists have attempted to relate the changes in work to human consciousness and activity [20, 21]. Early on, the debates focused on the effects of automation upon skill levels of workers and their collective sense of social identity [22] as well as on the nature of workplace socialization [23, 24]. More recently, the debate has shifted and can presently be characterized by the observation that "work is an educational site in which pedagogical and learning practices have always taken place" [25]. Two main viewpoints grow out of this characterization. The first is that responsibility for creating learning opportunities at work is a function of senior management [26, 27]. The other derives from ethnographic studies influenced by the Chicago School, claiming that "work serves as a primary site of socialization," and exploring the "hidden or unintentional outcomes of workplace socialization" rather than the purpose and structure of formal training and development programs [28-30]. Consequently, internship may be viewed not only as an approach to learning but as a process of socialization into official or unofficial workplace cultures.

Traditionally, the concept of internship as learning involves four main points:

- the intern as learner;
- the trade, occupation, or profession knowledge as fixed;
- the master as teacher;
- the idea that learning in the workplace is context bound, not conducive to transfer [31].

By extension, both classic cognitive psychology and educational anthropology tend to view internship as "lacking an explicit theory of instruction and not dependent upon formal teaching" [32-34]. And even studies that supported models of internship which embrace formal and informal learning within a variety of training opportunities provided by employers still concluded that interns and employers accord primary importance to acquiring professional knowledge and skill [35, 36].

Viewing internships as the basis for a social theory of learning requires moving beyond knowledge transmission and into learning processes and environments in which interns participate in "learning by doing" using the master or expert as a role model. This view abandons traditional approaches that considered internships as capable of being generalized to any profession; such approaches erroneously are based on the assumption that learning processes are invariant and the same for all occupations or professions. In reality, work contexts vary widely from some that are fairly routine and require only little specific knowledge to others that are extremely knowledge intensive; in other words, from contexts that are traditional-craft based to those that are constantly developing a body of theory for their profession [37]. Communications fields fall into the latter.

Collaborative practices mediate opportunities for learning. Because changes in knowledge and action are central to fields such as those found in communications industries, it follows that such changes are central to learning and the development of new forms of practice within those industries. This view also points out weaknesses in traditional conceptions of internship. For example, knowledge within such industries is socially constructed, and accordingly, interns become part of a work-based community of practice. Moreover, learning in such communities can be seen as a process that is enhanced by access to different communities of practice within the industry. As such fields develop (and certainly one can see this in communication industries), learners must increasingly relate the scientific concepts to the everyday experiences in order to make sense of their workplace practices and to solve problems that confront them there. Several studies have shown how resources that are external to communities of practice in conjunction with resources of learning technologies can be utilized to overcome internal contradictions that may appear within a professional field [38].

By focusing on commonalities between formal education and learning through internship experiences, one can resolve the contradictions that result from taking traditional approaches to internship, as well as the contradictions that arise in workplace experiences. Vygotsky's concept of the "zone of proximal development" [39] provides a useful tool in such an exploration. He defined it as

> the distance between the actual development level as determined by independent problem solving and the level of potential development as determined through problem solving under adult guidance or in collaboration with more able peers [39, p. 86].

This concept, Vygotsky's contribution to educational programs, attempts to provide a means by which learners could move beyond the levels of competence that they were capable of achieving on their own. Cole's work broadened this concept by suggesting that culture and cognition create each other within the zone through a dynamic relationship among people and social worlds that is expressed through language, art, and understanding [40].

Using these concepts as a foundation, internship becomes "the dynamic interrelationship between social, cultural, technological, and linguistic practices. . . . It creates a practice through which individuals and groups can learn over a period of time" [41].

The appeal that Vygotsky's theory and extensions of it have for the study of internships can be seen from the following:

> From a socio-cultural perspective, the basis of analysis [of learning] is no longer the properties of the individual, but the processes of socio-cultural activity, involving participation in socially constructed practices [42, p. 14].

Such an evolution from perspectives of personal levels of competence to socially constructed learning provides the basis to understanding internships as social institutions that are broadly applicable to a variety of modern professional contexts. Consequently, internships become a vehicle for "sociocultural transformation . . . between newcomers and old-timers in the context of a changing shared practice" [13, p. 49]. Authorities who hold this view conclude, therefore, that the relationship among learning, activity, and sociocultural contexts is mutually constitutive with communities of practice, and that expertise within a discipline is not reduced to the mastery of discrete tasks and skills. Rather, this view allows us to reconceptualize intelligence, insofar as it applies to knowledge within disciplines, as a distributed process rather than an attribute of individuals. Accordingly, zones of proximal development are populated by physical and cultural tools, as well as by other people; as these resources are brought to bear to shape human activity, it follows that intelligence and expertise are acquired through accomplishment rather than self-possession. While this does not deny that individuals develop forms of knowledge and skill, it presents and supports the collective basis through which individuals develop social identity, learn new forms of social practice, and become knowledgeable within a discipline; in other words, a process through which individuals develop the knowledge and skill required to operate successfully within a profession [13] and through which that profession develops. A social theory of learning is therefore established on the belief that the sum is in fact greater than its parts.

The implication of all this for a modern conceptualization of internships has to do with the developing belief that learning in the twenty-first century will increasingly become a matter of developing social relationships and identities within a profession. Internships will no longer be only experiences in which students acquire an on-the-job transfer of skills and knowledge; they will become (and are in fact in the process of becoming) experiences in which students can "reality-test" [43] ideas and principles learned in formal education. New forms of information technologies will continue to enhance these means of learning by creating opportunities for communities of practice to become distributed communities of learning. Such communities will extend the sources of information to which they have access, expand their sociocultural basis, and develop new forms of knowledgeability [44].

Providing students with opportunities to participate in workplace cultures through internships exposes them to the negotiated character of learning as a social practice in ways that are not yet readily applied in formal education, except perhaps in the necessarily artificial environment of participatory case studies; informs whether and how they will learn; and introduces them to opportunities to contribute to the production of new knowledge within the disciplines they have chosen.

SUMMARY

We have traced the foundations of work-to-learn experiences, which in this book, for clarity and consistency, will be called internships. It is clear from the long history of internships that, through those experiences, a sense of self-generating community is developed, communities into which interns are inculcated and through which they advance in their chosen professions. This evolution, in turn, is best described by social theories of learning and in particular Vygotsky's zone of proximal development [39], which can be traced to the present in such seminal works as those of Guile and Young [18] as well as Peter Senge [11]. Such foundations will form the basis for the explorations contained in the rest of this book.

REFERENCES

1. Aristotle, *Nicomachaean Ethics*, 1140a, 10-13, in *The Basic Works of Aristotle*, Richard McKeon (ed.). New York: Random House, 1941.
2. J. Dunne, *Back to the Rough Ground: Practical Judgment and the Lure of Technique*. Notre Dame, IN: University of Notre Dame Press, pp. 9-10, 1997.
3. S. F. Hamilton, *Apprenticeship for Adulthood*. New York: Macmillan, 1990.
4. R. Aldrich, The apprentice in history, in *Apprenticeship: Toward a New Paradigm of Learning*, P. Ainley and H. Rainbird (eds.). London: Kogan Page, 1999.
5. R. Farrell, *Women in Medieval Guilds*. www.virtualworldlets.net/Papers/Hosted/WomenMed.php
6. G. Clark, *English History*. Oxford: The Clarendon Press, 1971.
7. C. A. Prosser and T. H. Quigley, *Vocational Education in a Democracy*. Chicago: American Technical Society, 1949.
8. A. L. Rowse, *The England of Elizabeth*. New York: Macmillan, 1962.
9. R. I. Sutliffe, Revival of apprenticeship education in America, *ATEA Journal, 22*:4, pp. 7-10, April-May 1995.
10. G. Rikowski, Nietzche, Marx, and mastery: The learning unto death, in *Apprenticeship: Toward a New Paradigm of Learning*, P. Ainley and H. Rainbird (eds.). London: Kogan Page, 1999.
11. P. Senge, *The Fifth Discipline*. New York: Macmillan, 1995.
12. C. Sides, Community consensus and change in technical writing, in *Technical Communication Frontiers: Essays in Theory*, C. Sides, (ed.). St. Paul, MN: Association of Teachers of Technical Writing, pp. 1-14, 1994.
13. J. Lave, The practice of learning, in *Understanding Practice,* S. Chaiklen and J. Lave (eds.). Cambridge: Cambridge University Press, 1993.
14. J. Lave and E. Wenger, *Situated Learning*. Cambridge: Cambridge University Press, 1991.
15. Y. Engestrom, *Training for Change*. London: International Labour Office, 1995.
16. E. Fennell, Insight Comment. *Insight*, 31. Sheffield, UK: Employment Department Information Branch, 1994.
17. M. Young, Post-compulsory education and training in a learning society, *Australian and New Zealand Journal of Vocational Education Research, 3*:1, 1995.
18. D. Guile and M. Young, Apprenticeship as a conceptual basis for a social theory of learning, *Journal of Vocational Education and Training, 50*:2, 1998.
19. U. Beck, A. Giddens, and S. Lash, *Reflexive Modernisation*. Cambridge, UK: Policy Press, 1994.
20. A. Smith, *The Wealth of Nations*. Hammondsworth: Penguin Press, 1974.

21. K. Marx, Economic and philosophical manuscripts, in *The Marx-Engels Reader*, R. Tucker (ed.). New York: Norton, 1978.
22. R. Blauner, *Alienation and Freedom*. Chicago: University of Chicago Press, 1964.
23. H. Braverman, *Labor and Monopoly*. New York: Capital Monthly Review, 1974.
24. D. Noble, Social choice, in *Machine Design: The Case of Automatically Controlled Tools in Understanding Technology on Education*, H. Mackey, M. Young, and J. Benyon (eds.). London: Falmer Press, 1991.
25. C. Casey, *Work, Self, and Society*. London: Routledge, 1995.
26. H. Leymann and H. Kornbluh (eds.), *Socialisation and Learning at Work*. Aldershot, UK: Avesbury, Press, 1989.
27. E. Keep and K. Mayhew, Training policy for competitiveness: Time for a new perspective, in *Future Skill Demand and Supply*. London: PSI Publishing, 1995.
28. H. Becker, B. Greer, E. Hughes, and A. Strauss, *Boys in White: Student Culture in a Medical School*. Chicago: University of Chicago Press, 1961.
29. B. Geer (ed.), *Learning to Work*. London: Sage Publishing, 1972.
30. E. Hughes, *The Sociological Eye: Papers on Work, Self, and the Study of Society*. Chicago: Aldine Press, 1971.
31. D. Pratt, Concepts of teaching, *Adult Education Quarterly, 42*:4, pp. 207-220, 1992.
32. S. Schribner and M. Cole, Cognitive consequences of formal and informal learning, *Science, 82,* pp. 553-559, 1973.
33. A. Collins, S. J. Brown, and S. E. Newman, Cognitive apprenticeship, in *Knowledge, Learning, and Interaction: Essays in Honor of Robert Glaser,* L. B. Resnick (ed.). New Jersey: Erlbaum, 1989.
34. M. Coy, *Anthropological Perspectives on Apprenticeship*. New York: SUNY Press, 1989.
35. A. Brown, K. Evans, S. Blackman, and S. Germon, *Key Workers Technical Training and Mastery in the Workplace*. Bournemouth, UK: Hyde Publications, 1994.
36. A. Fuller, Modern apprenticeships process and learning: Some emerging issues, *Journal of Vocational Education and Research, 48,* pp. 229-249, 1996.
37. S. Gott, Rediscovering learning: Acquiring expertise in real-world problem-solving tasks, *Australian and New Zealand Journal of Vocational Education and Research, 3*:1, 1995.
38. Y. Engestrom, J. Viorkkunen, J. Helle, M. Pihlaja, and R. Poiketa, The change laboratory as a tool for transforming work, *Lifelong Learning in Europe, 2,* pp. 10-17, 1996.
39. L. S. Vygotsky, *Mind and Society*. Cambridge, UK: Cambridge University Press, 1978.
40. M. Cole, The zone of proximal development: Where culture and cognition create each other, in *Culture, Communication, and Cognition:*

Vygotskian Perspectives, J. Wertsch (ed.). New York: Cambridge University Press, 1985.
41. J. Lave, Teaching as learning in practice, *Mind, Culture, and Society, 3*:3, pp. 9-71, 1996.
42. B. Rogoff, *Apprenticeship in Thinking: Cognitive Development in Social Contexts*. New York: Oxford University Press, 1990.
43. L. DeNike, *Communication Media Internship Handbook*. Fitchburg, MA: Fitchburg State College Press, 1998.
44. D. Pea, Distributed Intelligence, in *Distributed Cognition*, G. Saloman (ed.). Cambridge, UK: Cambridge University Press, 1993.

CHAPTER 2

Internships As Learning Experiences

> Since we are an educational publishing company, our products are geared towards a specific audience, whether it be teachers or students, grade 1 or grade 12. Projects like these force the interns to really learn the design process, starting with recognizing the audience to following through by designing FOR the intended audience. Interns quickly learn that typography, layout, graphics, and design elements must all work together to create a successful publication.
>
> *Jessica Holland*
> *W. K Bradford Publishing*

Internships provide students with academic experiences that not only complement those resulting from standard classroom or seminar pedagogies but in many cases extend and improve upon them by engaging a broader variety of learning styles brought to the experiences by students and by practicably applying Vygotsky's zone of proximal development [1]. For example, much of what occurs in standard classroom or seminar environments is designed for linguistic/verbal learners. Instructional designers have recently recognized that not all students learn best in the same manner and have accordingly incorporated other learning styles into curriculum. But often these seem an uneasy fit, primarily because in most instances the person designing them is a linguistic learner himself or herself. Depending upon the professional field, however, internships naturally take advantage of almost all learning styles.

MULTIPLE-INTELLIGENCES MODEL OF LEARNING

Gardner's work on multiple intelligences posits at least seven different ways of learning, or in his terms, intelligences: kinesthetic, interpersonal, intrapersonal, logical, rhythmic, linguistic, and spatial [2]. Kinesthetic intelligence relates to movement and hands-on approaches to learning. Interpersonal intelligence relates to the relationships one creates with other persons and how learning occurs through those relationships; it is particularly helpful in groups working toward a common goal. Intrapersonal intelligence concerns inner states of being and self-awareness. Aristotle would connect it to the types of knowledge that accrue when a person is aware of art or craft done well—a self-actualizing knowledge associated with higher orders of thinking and reasoning. Logical intelligence is grounded in scientific thinking—induction, deduction, mathematics, pattern recognition—and the professions associated with it. Rhythmic intelligence is mostly related to musical matters, but also includes a sensitivity to sound that would be applicable in analysis used in other professions as well, such as certain types of automotive repair. Linguistic intelligence concerns learning through language. And spatial intelligence involves learning through image manipulations, awareness of space, graphic representations, and so forth. Clearly, each type of intelligence can be associated with certain professions that rely heavily upon it. But even more importantly, internships within those professions take into account—either by design or by happenstance—the types of learning that pre-professionals should expect to master as they proceed into and through their careers.

Much of classroom pedagogies is, by nature, bound to linguistic intelligence; internships provide avenues of access to other forms of intelligence, just as valid and just as valuable to twenty-first century professions.

Recognizing the similarities between formal educational pedagogies and service learning has been a surprisingly recent development; prior inquiries into internships as learning experiences have mostly focused on the differences between the two pedagogies. Simply put, such inquiries have traditionally envisioned typical classroom instruction as a transmission model of learning: the teacher instructs (sending the message) and the students learn (receiving the message). Internships, on the other hand, were typically viewed from the perspective of learn-by-experience models of instruction. It is Vygotsky's work, as well as the work of neo-Vygotskians, that effectively relates the two. Lave, in reconceptualizing internships as a basis for social theories of learning, points out that they emphasize the "dynamic, interrelationship between social, cultural, technological, and linguistic practices" [3]. They accordingly represent collective methods of learning; such an understanding of internships forms the theoretical foundation for this book.

Most simply stated, Vygotsky's zone of proximal development refers to the difference between what is learned and the ideal potential of what may be learned. Psychologists have interested themselves in the processes that occur within the zone, while educators have applied their studies in attempts to reduce the zone, facilitating learning experiences that would more closely approach the ideal. It is in the successes of this area of study that internships are finding a place of greater emphasis as pedagogic method. Much of the impetus for this research and its application comes from acknowledged limits of the usefulness of behavioral and cognitive theories with respect to understanding learning [2-4]. As a result, more and more psychologists are turning to an examination of how learning is developed not only by individuals and through individualistic practices but also by groups and through group practices. The growth of this interest seems particularly fueled by a perceived failure of rationalism to account for the relationships among social context, cognition, and pedagogy [5], as well as by dissatisfaction with pedagogies that require presenting concepts abstracted from the environment in which they are learned and, especially, used [6-8]. In other words, individualistic, reason-based assessments of learning are not enough to account for what occurs educationally within the context of internships; "culturalist" perspectives, based on an increasing understanding of group learning, are now thought to more accurately describe such educational experiences.

This evolution to culturalist perspectives of cognition provides the foundation for viewing internships as a basis of a social theory of learning, bringing about a shift from understanding internships strictly as "social institutions" devoted only to traditional craft and technical skills to understanding internships and learning as inextricably linked in ways that are more broadly applicable to modern professions [9]. Experiential learning in group-based structural environments can now be seen as more than a rich learning environment; it is one in which the proverbial sum is greater than its individual parts.

CULTURE, LEARNING, AND THE ZONE OF PROXIMAL DEVELOPMENT

The importance of Vygotsky's work to internships lies in the connections between sociocultural transformation and the relationships of newcomers and established experts in professional fields [10]. These communities of shared practice represent the environments for which students are educated and into which all educational institutions hope their graduates will proceed upon the completion of their academic careers.

Taking a societal perspective on the zone of proximal development allows educators to focus on the social aspects of learning. It reveals the important differences between what individuals do daily and the new forms of knowledge that groups of practitioners must create in order to solve emerging problems and remain competitive in an increasingly fast-evolving global marketplace. Four orientations have surfaced:

- How social structures and social relationships influence learning over time
- The importance of relationships among communities of practice
- The opportunities for learning within such communities
- The human and technological resources that support learning [11]

Traditionally, internships were seen as a method of conserving established practices within a profession. A social view of learning sees internships as mutually constitutive, developing new forms of knowledge through the interrelationship of learning, professional activities, and cultural contexts over a period of time. This leads to reconceptualizing intelligence as a distributed process over and through a culture rather than only as the attributes of discrete individuals. Accordingly, the zone of proximal development, particularly as it applies to internships, is replete with persons, cultural tools, and resources that can come together in an application to shape learning and direct human activity. As a result, what we have traditionally viewed as learning—the combination of intelligence and expertise—can now be seen as being developed through practical accomplishment rather than a building up of a body of self-possessed knowledge. It is, as the introduction of this book noted, learning by doing—education put to use.

SITUATED LEARNING THEORY

As early as 1929, noted British philosopher Alfred North Whitehead railed against traditional methods of education—the teaching of "inert knowledge" [12] that would prove to be incapable of application when students needed to do so in order to solve problems encountered in real-life scenarios. Situated Learning Theory provides a solution to such problems associated with traditional pedagogies. According to the theory, "knowledge and skills are learned in the contexts that reflect how knowledge is obtained and applied in everyday situations" [13]. Situated cognition, therefore, describes learning as a sociocultural phenomenon. Consequently, in pedagogies based on this theory, participation in the real activities of daily living is a practice that constitutes and informs learning. Subject matter, as it exists from discipline to discipline, becomes embedded in these ongoing experiences. Participation in the activities creates opportunities for learners to develop—in communion with colleagues with greater knowledge and experience—by facing and overcoming real-world challenges. This becomes a method of instruction that extends beyond the experiential activities designed into such activities as case studies; it become real to the learner because it is. Learners see their entry into and progress within a discipline linked to the knowledge they can obtain and apply directly to their chosen professions [14].

According to Lave and Wenger [11], to situate learning is to place it in a particular setting in which the thinking and doing processes used by experts to accomplish knowledge and skill tasks are available to learners. Most situated learning theorists conclude that learning, according to this perspective, has four major components:

1. It is located in the actions of everyday situations.
2. Knowledge is acquired through situations and transfers to similar situations.

3. Learning is the result of social processes that include ways of thinking, perceiving, problem solving, and interacting with others and the environment, in addition to traditional forms of declarative and procedural knowledge.
4. Knowledge is not separated from experience but exists in social environments comprised of persons, activities, and environments [11].

Learning, accordingly, becomes that which is not separated from the hurly-burly of daily interactions, but that which incorporates it in all its complexity and richness. Learning becomes the processes by which learners and experts participate together to solve problems involving intellectual and psychomotor skills [14]. Lave describes this as occurring in two stages: "way in" and "practice" [15]. Way in describes the probationary period in which the learner (or in our application, the intern) observes experts performing their professional work. After a substantial period of becoming enculturated to the profession, the learner then begins, with guidance and mentoring, to participate, embarking on his or her own career path to excellence. Practice, therefore, becomes the way to refine and perfect knowledge.

As has been pointed out, internships designed in such a way as to take advantage of situated cognition approaches to learning create a social environment in which experts and learners participate together in a social organization to solve problems related to their professions—communities of practice. Situated learning should inculcate reflective thinking on the part of the learner. It is not enough for persons to merely understand what they are doing, they must place that understanding within the context of knowing *why* they do it in certain ways and to consider ways in which to improve it. The richness of communities of practice makes it more likely for this to occur.

As more communities of practice develop intrinsic forms of knowledge within their sociocultural environment—knowledge that is both professional and cultural—it becomes more necessary to examine and understand the relationships among such communities. By understanding these relationships, we are more likely able to extend communally developed learning across broader networks of communities within a society. Activity, meaning, cognition, knowing, and learning must be viewed in relation to each other.

> Learning is not a special mental process. Rather, it is a relational matter, generated in social living, historically, in social formations whose participants engage with each other as a condition and precondition for existence [16].

Hence, learning, while it doesn't diminish the importance of professional competency, becomes more a matter of developing relationships and identities within communities of practice in which those competencies are exercised. Applied to internships, this perspective is radically different from the more traditional view of internships as a means of transferring knowledge and skills to the next generation of professionals. In the past, skills transfer referred to the ability of students to take what was learned in academic environments out into the workplace and apply it there. But within professional contexts, in which the half-life of knowledge (that period of time in which one-half of what one knows has become obsolete) is shorter than the typical college undergraduate career, such traditional views of learning are doomed to failure. Rather, successful students are those who learn how to learn—those who are not bound by traditionally accepted competencies but who are inquisitive, constantly searching for new and effective answers to problems that confront them [9]. If they establish this approach to learning in the academic community of practice, it is more readily transferable to the professional community. And it is through internships that students are able to test their perceptions of learning, their suitability for a particular profession, and their likelihood of success in it.

This "reality testing" [17] and the communal learning associated with it, however, do not occur in a vacuum. They are supported by vital human and technological resources to create environments in which interns and professionals can see ways in which it might be both possible and necessary to create new knowledge. This happens consistently across disciplines, but one example from the authors' experience will suffice to demonstrate it. A graduate of our department in the early 1990s entered the film industry in computer animation. Being unsatisfied with the technological resources and their limitations at the time, he developed new software and consequently received an Academy Award for technical excellence in 2003. Persons who excel in their chosen field stand out—from Academy Awards to Nobel prizes; but such developments (though certainly not all lead to such notice) are more commonplace than one might assume. Persons working in various communities of practice consistently come up with new ways of doing things, new approaches to old problems, and innovative solutions to new ones.

Internships, seen in such light, become transformatory experiences. If the zone of proximal development can be used to describe social learning contexts, then knowledge is collective and can be the basis for transforming sociocultural contexts, cognition, and practice.

COLLECTIVE INTELLIGENCE

If one accepts the last sentence of the previous section, as we do, then it is imperative to examine an emerging scholarly discipline that some find promising and others troubling. If situated learning creates communities of practice in which knowledge can be seen as collective, then this defines collective intelligence, and internships—so conceived—are avenues into it.

Douglas Engelbart and others define collective intelligence as "a working form of intelligence which overcomes groupthink and individual cognitive bias in order to allow a collective to cooperate on one process—while maintaining reliable intellectual performance" [18]. Another collective intelligence theorist extends the definition of this phenomenon by describing it as "the capacity of a human community to evolve toward higher order complexity thought, problem-solving, and integration through collaboration and innovation" [18]. Many of these theorists reside in the artificial-intelligence discipline, but virtually all agree that collective intelligence is, at its root, a human enterprise. It is based (and has been for longer than most people realize) on a willingness to share, on similar mindsets, and on a belief that openness to the value of distributed intelligence functions for the common good. In this sense, therefore, tribes formed on such collective bases long before the dawn of recorded history.

In twenty-first-century applications, including those in which internships fall, individuals who respect collective intelligence do not sacrifice their individuality; rather, they bring their individualities to the collective, confident in those individual abilities, while recognizing that indeed the sum is greater than its individual parts. Accordingly, maximizing collective intelligence involves a community of practice being open to accepting and developing potential input from any member. A case in point can be taken from our recent internship experience. One of our photography interns at a high-end Manhattan commercial photography studio was encouraged to experiment with a new $55,000 Hasselblad digital-medium format camera. The student owned a low-end film-based Hasselblad, but had not previously used the top-of-the-line digital version. He figured out a method of taking readings from various regions of the visible light spectrum, exposing an image three times within those ranges and, as a result, created a two-dimensional image that, when printed, was so lifelike that it appeared to have three-dimensional textures. That method is now being incorporated into the studio and in other studios as well, as it makes its way across the commercial photography community of practice.

One might ask, isn't this the same process that has been used for decades and which individuals use to patent their ideas, form companies, and make fortunes? Yes, but with one key difference: the intern *shared* his discovery. Collective intelligence enthusiasts [19, 20] point out that from the Industrial Revolution through a little less than a generation ago, schools and corporations separated elites from the persons expected to follow them. Organizations valued secrecy, bureaucracy, and compartmentalized knowledge. This, such experts claim, is pathological thinking that enables selfish decisions to be made against the public interest, and as many news reports have pointed out in their coverage of CEOs raiding the corporate treasury, even against the interests of noncollective communities of practice. Collective intelligence, these experts believe, restores the power of people over society and communities of practice and neutralizes the power of vested interests that manipulate information in order to concentrate wealth. There is more and more circumstantial evidence that the generation of young people entering their careers in the early twenty-first century—connected to each other 24/7 through blogs, mobile internet technologies, text messaging, and so forth—find the openness of collective societies appealing. And they have welcomed wholeheartedly without question the technologies that make such societies not only possible, but unavoidable.

Collaborative activity, by necessity, reconfigures the workplace [21]. One of the more fascinating recent developments of analyzing the transformed workplace is Szuba'a work [22]. He proposes a mathematical method for modeling collective intelligence. It is presumed to be an unconscious, random, parallel, and distributed computational process that runs in mathematical logic determined by its inherent social structure. While the mathematics of this model are far beyond the scope of this book, some of its applications are important to viewing how internships work to permit entry into professions. In this model, beings and information are conceived as abstract information units carrying expressions of mathematical logic. They are "quasi-randomly displacing" other information units as they interact with the environment and other persons or information. This interaction creates multithread inference processes, which we perceive as collective intelligence. Simply put, according to this modeling and the understanding that is at its foundation, collective intelligence is a nearly random method of acquiring and replacing information as individuals interact with other individuals, environment, and information in a community of practice. Therefore, collective intelligence is the property of social structures, and methods are already in development for measuring its effectiveness in a wide range of organizational and corporate entities.

But as mentioned at the outset of this section, not everyone welcomes these ideas, and some see them as outright threatening to what they perceive as inherent human individualism. Does the embrace of situated learning, communities of practice, and collective intelligence lead to the hive-mind scenarios that are well-depicted in science fiction? It is too soon to tell. However, no less a figure than former Vice President of the United States Al Gore has suggested that "the U.S. Constitution is a program that lets us all do together what we could not do separately" [23], and not too many people would find that notion threatening.

CONCLUSION

Internships are the transitional experience into a transformed professional environment founded on situated cognition, communities of practice, and collective intelligence. Pedagogical approaches to internships should view them as a form of situated learning in which interns can be sensitized to the "negotiated character of learning as social practice" [4]. As opportunities for students to participate in communities of practice of professional cultures, internships have a strong influence on what and how the student learns. But transformative learning, as with all other forms of learning, still has to be designed for it to be effective. Instructional design in this case, however, should focus more on the social processes, relationships, and resources that interns will encounter and need in order to support learning. Instruction must ensure that the goals of learning through internships are clear and that, in the best cases, participants are encouraged to think beyond the immediate. Only this can reliably predict that the zone of proximal development is collectively organized to facilitate the transformation of sociocultural context, cognition, and practice. It is applicable to academic learning environments, to professional workplace cultures, and to the links between the two that internships provide.

REFERENCES

1. L. S. Vygotsky, *Mind and Society*. Cambridge: Cambridge University Press, 1978.
2. H. Gardner, *Frames of Mind: The Theory of Multiple Intelligences*. New York: Basic Books, 1983.
3. J. Lave, The practice of learning, in *Understanding Practice*, S. Chaiklen and J. Lave (eds.). Cambridge: Cambridge University Press, 1993.
4. Y. Engestrom, *Training for Change*. London: International Labor Office, 1995.
5. J. Wertsch (Ed.), *Culture Communication and Cognition: Vygotskian Perspectives*. New York: Cambridge University Press, 1985.
6. S. L. Starr, Working together: Symbolic interactionism, activity theory, and information systems, in *Cognition and Communication at Work*, D. Middleton and Y. Engestrom (eds.), Cambridge: Cambridge University Press, 1996.
7. S. Billett, Constructing vocational knowledge: Histories, communities, and ontology, *Journal of Vocational Education and Training, 48*, pp. 141-154, 1996.
8. D. Layton, Science education as praxis: The relationship of school science to practical action studies, *Science Education, 19,* pp. 42-79, 1991.
9. J. Lave, Teaching as learning in practice, *Mind, Culture, and Society, 3*:3, pp. 9-71, 1996.
10. D. Guile and M. Young, Apprenticeship as a conceptual basis for a social theory of learning, *Journal of Vocational Education and Training, 50*:2, pp. 173-192, 1998.
11. J. Lave and E. Wenger, *Situated Learning*. Cambridge: Cambridge University Press, 1991.
12. A. N. Whitehead, *The Aims of Education and Other Essays*. New York: The Free Press, 1929.
13. D. Stein, *Situated Learning in Adult Education*. ERIC Digest No. 195, Columbus, OH, 1998.
14. J. R. Anderson, L. M. Reder, and H. A. Simon, Situated learning and education, *Educational Researcher, 25*:4, pp. 5-11, 1996.
15. J. Lave, The culture of acquisition and the practice of understanding, in *Situated Cognition: Social, Semiotic, and Psychological Perspectives,*

D. Kirschner and J. Whitson (eds.). Mahwah, NJ: Lawrence Erlbaum Associates, pp. 17-35, 1997.

16. B. Lankard, *New Ways of Learning in the Workplace.* ERIC Digest No. 161, Columbus, OH, 1995.
17. P. Senge, *The Fifth Discipline: The Art and Practice of the Learning Organization*. New York: Doubleday, 1990.
18. D. Engelbart, *Leveraging Our Collective Intelligence.* Stanford University Colloquium <www.bootstrap.org/colloquium/session_03/session_03.html>
19. G. Por, The quest for collective intelligence, in *Community Building: Renewing Spirit and Learning in Business*. London: New Leaders Press, 1995.
20. H. Rheingold, *Smart Mobs*. Cambridge, MA: Perseus Publishing, 2002.
21. R. D. Steele, *The New Craft of Intelligence*. Oakton, VA: Oss Press, 2002.
22. T. Szuba, *Computational Collective Intelligence*. New York: Wiley, 2001.
23. A. Gore, *Earth in the Balance.* New York: Penguin, 1993.

CHAPTER 3

Internships As Professional Experiences

> Interns play a key role in our organization. They act as support, entry-level account executives. They come to meetings, go through the entire process on a project, and, as often as possible, we try to give them a start-to-finish project so that they leave our agency at the end of their internship with a complete project recap in their portfolio.
>
> *Anne-Marie Aigner*
> *Aigner Associates*

Many benefits, both tangible and intangible, accrue to corporations and other organizations when they host an intern. The following are some of the tangible benefits, but they can also be grouped to some extent under the broader and less tangible category of social theories of learning by seeing them within the context of how the growth of individuals contributes to the growth and development of institutions:

- contributing to the growth of a profession
- gaining knowledge of what is being taught in academic programs
- accessing new ideas, skills, and training for the organization
- expanding the networking base of the organization
- developing relationships with academic institutions
- coaching and influencing young careers
- developing and exercising supervisory skills

- expanding time and opportunities for special projects
- procuring extra help
- engaging in pre-employment screening.

Certainly there are costs to hosting an intern as well, but those will be discussed in a later chapter. This chapter will examine the benefits.

CONTRIBUTING TO THE GROWTH OF A PROFESSION

Successful organizations that reconceive themselves as learning organizations in the twenty-first century will consciously devote efforts, which extend beyond profitability, to the conservation and growth of their professions. Internships and internship supervisors have a major role to play in this. Many supervisors report that they enjoy the teaching role that hosting an intern allows them. This kind of mentoring and the sharing of information that it provides gives them an opportunity in one-on-one relationships with the next generation of professionals to contribute back to the profession that has nurtured them. Providing for others to learn from the successes, challenges, mistakes, and even the blind alleys they've explored heightens their awareness of their professional value and provides an opportunity for them to process their own career journeys as they share those experiences with the next generation. Doing so fosters a sense of success that extends beyond a single career or even lifetime, for it permits internship supervisors to witness the responsibilities and contributions they have made to a profession, and consequently to the society in which that profession exists. Mentoring interns from such a perspective often brings out the nurturing teacher in many internship site supervisors. As Elise Kaplan, an internship supervisor at Commercial Ware of Natick, Massachusetts, reported about the personal and professional responsibility she feels in mentoring interns, ". . . after considering all the rational reasons for supporting interns within our company, in the end, 'I just like to do it'" [1].

In most academic institutions, interns have spent between two and five (or more) years studying the field of their choice. They are prepared to make the transition into that field, and internships provide students an important first step in that transitional process. Importantly, many internship site supervisors report that a vital part of their own education included internship experiences that were rich and valuable to their career development. When asked why they support interns now that they are themselves successful in their careers, they suggest that part of their motivation is an attitude of providing for others the same opportunities they were fortunate enough to enjoy. When asked about this sense of responsibility to ensuing generations of communications professionals, Andrew Cunningham of the Tufts University School of Veterinary Medicine in North Grafton, Massachusetts, replied that he "appreciated [his] experience [as an intern] and . . . wanted to help out" [2]. That prevailing sense of professional obligation runs throughout the research conducted for this book. It is a primary basis for understanding internships in terms of how they contribute to the growth of a profession.

Much of formal, post-high-school education, particularly in liberal and applied arts fields, lacks the context that young professionals need. Often students at college and university levels are left wondering how what they study relates to the professions that await them upon graduation. Legal, medical, and teaching professions have long recognized this and, as was pointed out in the Introduction, have for centuries incorporated field experiences into their informal and formal approaches used to prepare the next generation of professionals. Their ongoing success in utilizing learn-by-doing instructional methods provides an accessible (if unintended) longitudinal study of an important way to fully acquaint students with the application and full context of material learned in the formal academic settings. Even when academic instructors attempt to replicate real-world experience with case studies and client projects, for students and for teachers alike, these remain at their foundation, replications. Not until would-be professionals begin to live the occupational life they have chosen (and we would advocate that they begin this as interns) do they really start to understand how their formal knowledge will be applied. Because the context and professional environment that internships provide are absolutely real, they function as profoundly valuable experiences.

The following is a case in point. One of the authors' recent interns was placed at Turner Sports Marketing in Atlanta. On the young woman's first day, her supervisor told her that she "planned to treat [the intern] as she would any other entry-level employ" [3], meaning that the intern would be assigned to one of the division's clients and mentored through the process of developing marketing and promotional materials for that client. "Your client for the next four months," the intern was told, "is the Atlanta Braves." A lot of people learn best by doing. Internships give young professionals the opportunity to do that, particularly when what they are doing is work that is actually valued by the host organization. Their experiences on the job, contributing to projects at hand, produce a confidence in their professional abilities that only such experiences can foster. The give and take of the situation described above clearly reminds us of how the internship experience is deeply rooted in the social theories of learning. In the Introduction to *Mind and Society*, Michael Cole and Sylvia Scribner write, "According to Vygotsky . . . the mechanism for individual developmental change is rooted in society and culture" [4, p. 7]. The culture of an organization also plays a role in the learning process of interns. Many aspects of social-learning theory are present in the assignment given to this particular intern. She would experience the upward spiral of learning and development that is Vygotsky's zone of proximal development; in other words, what persons "can do with the assistance of others might in some sense be even more indicative of their mental development than what they can do alone" [4, p. 84]. The intern will be receiving some assistance from her supervisor, but clearly through this process she will come to realize what she still needs to learn, and one can expect her to use such knowledge as motivation and direction for continued learning advancement.

Internship site hosts also teach interns through role modeling, as has been the case throughout history. Simply by being present, interns learn and are indoctrinated in a wide range of the professional "mysteries" of their chosen discipline:

- the common approaches to projects within the discipline
- the attitude professionals within the discipline exhibit toward their work
- the ways in which clients and customers are treated
- the current state and ongoing development of disciplinary theory and philosophy
- the work ethic and work flow common to the discipline.

What interns learn in such experiences is (and should be) transferable, allowing them to compare and contrast one place of work and even a particular profession to another. Once again, this is a key concept of viewing the role of internships in learning organizations.

By relation and extension, another aspect of internship hosts as role models is their ability to model their own continued professional development. In some internship experiences, interns have the opportunity to attend their first professional development meeting conducted by an association or training organization that serves their profession. Encouraging interns to participate in such activities—particularly encouraging them to join the professional societies in their fields—is also a means by which internships further the growth of the profession. Interns who witness professionals attending conferences, reading professional magazines, and independently researching topics to learn new material or techniques that will be useful to them in the future, learn early and firsthand that successfully holding professional positions in virtually any discipline requires one to be a lifelong learner. This is perhaps the most valuable aspect of providing the real professional environment that internships afford, as well as being the foundation for viewing internships in relation to their effect on professional growth.

GAINING KNOWLEDGE OF WHAT IS BEING TAUGHT IN ACADEMIC INSTITUTIONS

From time to time we hear generalized comments that education is not meeting the needs of the business community, that the educational institutions are not teaching the materials or concepts that are needed in entry-level employees. Many at those same educational institutions take this feedback lightly because they maintain that they are not only attempting to prepare students to be employees but to prepare them, as well, for rewarding and successful lives in general. Educators know they cannot prepare each student for the specifics of each work site. But conversely, too often business interests do not know fully what is being taught in schools. Hosting interns can help create two-way communication between both enterprises and thereby foster a linkage between what is taught in academic institutions and what is needed in the future employees of the business community. As a result, business and industry learn about what is being taught in academia by becoming directly involved in the professional preparation of students. From this knowledgeable vantage point, their comments and constructive criticism become more valuable to academic institutions.

For example, internship site supervisors are frequently able to influence the curriculum of the schools from which they host interns because they are in an important position as both mentors to would-be professionals and as representatives of the disciplines within which they work. They provide academic institutions with feedback on how the product of their curriculum, the graduating student, is meeting their needs. A specific case in point: one site supervisor, Robert Brown of Genzyme, with whom the authors of this book have frequently worked, has spoken of our department's curriculum on several occasions [4]. He has the added benefit of also being a graduate of the program from which he now hosts interns. He would like to see the program incorporate a stronger focus on business and corporate communications than currently seems to be the trend within the department. His and other comments repeatedly find their way back to the department and into ongoing discussions of curriculum, program design, course selection, equipment purchases, and other related areas.

Some academic institutions adopt a more regulated approach to these two-way communications by having formal advisory committees from the professional community that assist the institution in considering the difficult choices involved in curriculum design. But even for institutions that adopt a less formal approach, site supervisors serve as a relevant check on how departments, programs, and entire institutions are meeting the needs of future employers. If they find students lacking, especially when compared with students from other schools with similar programs of study, they can provide important feedback to stimulate curriculum change. That being said, it is important for business and industry representatives to remember (often perhaps from their own experience) that not all students always learn everything taught in a program. Given that, internships nonetheless provide an opportunity for professionals within a discipline to assess and correct any shortcomings they find in interns in order to better prepare them for successful entry into their chosen careers, as well as to understand what is being taught at academic institutions and make valuable comments regarding the academic programs from which their interns come.

ACCESSING NEW IDEAS, SKILLS, AND TRAINING

As we have seen, internship sites often influence the content of courses and programs in academic institutions, but at other times the reverse is also true. Students can bring new knowledge and ideas into corporate environments. The primary responsibility for most interns is to learn their new field. Professionals already in the field have full-time responsibilities devoted to other enterprises, from managing projects to delivering products and services to a customer base. These often do not leave as much time as one might wish for activities considered as important aspects of becoming lifelong learners. However, interns can at times aid established professionals by importing new capabilities and knowledge to the corporate environments.

Recently one of the authors saw this firsthand with regard to multimedia and the use of the Internet. At a particular internship host site, the intern was clearly going to be the person who had the most background and knowledge in Web site design and management. Up to the point of hosting this intern, the site had contracted with an outside vendor to do their Web work. A highly skilled intern allowed the company to save money while not losing productivity. However, this type of situation can create challenges for even the most skilled interns, as they do not have a mentor at their internship site to turn to. The particular student involved in this instance knew this as he had sought out the site on his own. He contacted the organization and proposed it to the school as the place he would like to do his internship. While on internship, if he encountered a problem he could not solve, he called his former instructors at the college. This worked to some extent, but in retrospect, his frustration level was higher in general than it probably would have been if he'd had a mentor at the site. We have also witnessed the occasional situation in which interns are placed in environments wherein they have stronger skills than some of the employees, resulting in employees being dismissed and the intern being hired at the conclusion of the internship. While this is rare and probably not completely desirable, it does happen. A more common experience involves professional jealousy; one in particular comes to mind. The intern's knowledge of certain software packages was so much more advanced than that of other professional employees at her site that she was asked to provide training in the use of those programs, bypassing the full-time employee who was responsible for this. In both of these instances, the interns had to draw upon barely developed interpersonal skills and use them in a professional environment to which they had just been introduced in order to diminish the unavoidable discomfort that was felt by all persons involved. To their credit, both were successful at doing so.

While these specific circumstances are thankfully rare, it is relatively common for internship sites to experience interns as a source of fresh, new, enthusiastic ideas. Interns provide a pair of eyes to which everything is new and nothing is by necessity the "way it has always been done." The presence of interns contributes a new ingredient to the host site and provides access not only to fresh enthusiasm but to state-of-the-art knowledge and skill. As such, interns can be seen as an important resource for the organization that hosts them.

EXPANDING THE NETWORKING BASE OF THE ORGANIZATION

Even when interns are not hired by the hosting organization, they develop a history and a relationship with that organization that can be kept alive. Such connections and professional friendships create and expand a network that is mutually beneficial for the intern or new professional and the internship host alike. For instance, after interns leave a host organization, they might obtain positions with other companies while still maintaining relationships with the people who hosted their internship. From such a relationship there can develop a level of shared information (presuming, of course, that such information is not proprietary) and experiences that can broaden the profession at large. The expanded network that a professional entity develops through hosting an intern can be beneficial to that entity long after the intern has left. One example, a well-known advertising photography studio in Manhattan, stands out. This studio, the co-owner of which graduated from the authors' department, regularly hosts our interns. Following internship, the studio maintains a close relationship with their former interns, using them as paid professionals and providing them with ongoing experience and growth that have successfully launched several photographic careers. So successful, in fact, that every intern who wished to remain and work in the advertising photography industry in New York City has been able to do so.

In long-established internship programs such as ours, former interns, who later host interns, frequently use their professional friendships with other former interns and host sites to provide job counseling to new professionals or to provide leads to companies who might be hiring and looking for a particularly well-qualified person to fill a position. The use of such networks benefits interns as well as host sites. At another internship site in the film industry, where we have placed interns for years, these networks have led to remarkable opportunities, including a circumstance in which five former graduates worked on the same Academy Award winning film.

DEVELOPING RELATIONSHIP WITH ACADEMIC INSTITUTIONS

It has already been mentioned that the feedback internship sites can provide to academic institutions regarding their preparation of students is a valuable influence on curriculum development. A continuing relationship between academic institutions and internship sites can prove beneficial for the corporation in that the more the school comes to know the host site, its supervisors, its mission, and its mode of operation, the better the position the school is in to provide the right match between interns and the host sites. This matching process is key in putting the most successful components of an internship experience together. Frank and open exchanges of information allow for the likelihood that this matching will be as successful as possible. As a result, our experience has been that internship management is a continuous enterprise. Regardless of whether or not a site is hosting an intern in any given semester, we are in constant communication with our regularly used internship sites, exploring feedback regarding the interns we have placed there in the recent past and communicating that feedback to faculty and administrators so that it can be incorporated quickly and successfully into the curriculum.

COACHING AND INFLUENCING A YOUNG CAREER

Internships are important times of transition. Interns are embarking on preprofessional experiences that will help them bridge between academic preparation and the professional training required for employment. Students usually choose specific internship sites because they believe the site provides the entry into their chosen professional niche. Internship sites offer real-life experience, but they also offer a host of role models within the organization that interns can connect with, emulate, or reject. As a result, internships are incredibly rich learning environments that provide opportunities for established professionals to directly influence the growth of the intern. They differ in this respect from academic experiences, particularly in the amount of one-to-one mentoring that is available between professional and intern. For example, in typical college academic experiences, one professor interacts with 15 to 30 or more students in a classroom or lecture hall, but in internships there may be several people in the department that the student intern can learn from one-on-one. Again, social learning theories and Vygotsky's zone of proximal development come into play. Internships provide a rich opportunity for this type of development. For example, some of our best and most frequently used sites, in recognition of the educational component of internship, design problems for interns to solve, mentor them through the solution process, and evaluate the results. This takes significant amounts of time and demonstrates a site supervisor's commitment to hosting an internship; more importantly, it provides significant growth experiences for the would-be professionals—experiences they will take to their first paying position in the discipline.

Student/teacher ratios at an internship, as a result, are inverted from what students have experienced in their respective academic institutions. There is usually much more contact time between supervisors and interns than has been available between students and professors in academic courses. Typically in college courses, students interact with professors in class for 3 hours a week for 10 to 15 weeks, depending on whether the institution uses the quarter or semester system. That experience approximates a total of 30 to 45 hours for the semester. In the first week of a full-time internship, many interns reach that level of contact with the internship site and with individuals at the site. Moreover, sites excel in validating what interns have heard and been taught prior to internship. And in virtually all experiences we have seen, sites and the professionals there have a uniquely open-minded person in the intern, who is eager to absorb as much as possible about the new learning environment, creating what has rightly been termed a "teachable moment" [5].

Another aspect that strengthens this teachable moment attitude is that internship sites often provide a much narrower focus than most courses that are taught at the undergraduate level. As a result, interns often select a site because of its focus and the professional direction students wish to pursue. Academic institutions, on the other hand, attempt to provide a wide, stable base of professional training on which students can later build. For example, students who have studied video and film production may eventually want to go into casting for such productions. They may have done some casting for student productions, and casting may have been covered in a general way in some of their production classes. But the specialized nature of internships requires that such potential interns give their placement considerable thought and that they decide on a specialization within the broader profession they seek to enter. As a result, when that intern who is interested in casting decides to obtain an internship at a casting company where the people who own and manage the company have been in the business for years, the student will be more likely to absorb as much of the information and nuances of that specific business as is possible. The process of deciding what they want brings them to a critical maturation point in their career at which they are ready to fully engage and commit themselves. Academic institutions can only rarely offer the level of specialized training (at the undergraduate level) that a carefully chosen internship site can.

Internships are also a special time in students' lives because they often occur near the end of their college careers. While graduation may have been anxiously anticipated for a number of years, as it approaches, there is often a shift toward thinking more about what the graduate's work life will be like after graduation. Work prior to graduation has, for many students, been schoolwork mixed with some part-time paid employment. Many students find renewed will and drive to continue and excel in their school work when they stop to compare their future careers with their part-time jobs. Such contemplation adds to their willingness to be prepared to hear and learn from their internship sites.

Many students may also hope that their internship site, if the students' experience is positive, will provide them with their first professional position. This additional aspect of internships persuades students to take on the attitude, to some extent, of new employees who are in a probationary period. As a result, they take especial care to impress internship hosts and meet their perceived professional needs. Conversely, internship supervisors and co-workers usually make significant impressions on interns. William Ramsey confirms this and states, "Often the interpersonal relations that develop between supervisors and students are among the most significant part of the students' experience" [5, p. 250]. Students have chosen a professional setting they believe will help them to develop their academic specialty. Internship sites demonstrate to interns, through the work and reputation of supervisors and colleagues, the richness of what interns can learn at the site, as well as the extent to which they can eventually grow as professionals themselves.

There are exceptions to this, however. These usually occur when the site or the student settles for something different than what each was seeking. This often negates the positive expectations that both the intern and site initially held. Consequently, it is important for both parties in the internship experience to carefully prepare for the selection and placement of interns. That can be a critical aspect of mentoring young careers.

One of the reasons for this is that with a positive beginning, an important career-development maturation point can be reached early, allowing certain types of synergy to occur. These include the rewards of seeing one's academic work bear fruit in one's chosen profession and an understanding that success and professional growth require continuous lifelong learning. Because of the synergy available through internships, many interns report a perception of enormous amounts of learning taking place on internship. Over 50% of the authors' students report that they learned more on their internship in 3 months than they did in their academic experiences over a period of 3½ years or more. It is important to realize, however, (whether interns recognize it or not) that those 3+ years of academic experience prepared them for the learning they obtained at their internship sites.

Another result of the amount of contact between interns and professionals at internship sites is that by the end of an internship, site supervisors and co-workers know their interns professionally better than perhaps anyone else. They have gotten to know them as individuals and as would-be professionals. They have worked with them enough to observe their strengths and weaknesses. This unique vantage point, when coupled with the broader experience and perspective that supervisors bring to internships, provides for the coaching opportunities that are particularly important to internships. Coaching and the advice and constructive feedback available at sites are uniquely valuable to interns. Students, even near the end of their academic careers, can rarely imagine the range of directions that their careers could take. But through exposure to the professional-life stories of the people at the site, they are able to gain a broader perspective on career paths, which may serve to further their confidence, as well as to stimulate their thinking with regard to the responsibilities for their own professional growth.

And this kind of coaching can be rewarding for sites and supervisors as well. While coaching develops better performance and increased confidence levels in interns, it also validates the experience and knowledge of supervisors.

Perhaps one of the most valuable aspects of influencing young careers occurs for those students who embark on their internships with overinflated perceptions of their knowledge and skills. They have nearly completed the academic portion of their professional preparation, they have been diligently studying and learning in academic institutions for years, and they may have received good grades in the process. However, it is when they arrive at an internship site that they realize how much more there is to learn. This component of the need-to-know factor has been mentioned specifically by Vygotsky. When he describes the practical implications of the overview of the developmental history of written language, he indicates that "teaching . . . entails a second requirement that it be 'relevant to life,' that what is to be learned 'becomes necessary'" [4, p. 118]. This seems to be exactly how the verisimilitude of the internship experience is intrinsically motivating to interns. Conscientious supervisors provide an invaluable service to such interns in gently leading them to new plateaus of knowledge. The result of this mutually supportive environment is that the confidence levels of interns—even those who arrived overconfident—may increase exponentially, building reserves from which the future professional may have to draw during a career's inevitable difficult times. If supervisors can, by their honest coaching and feedback, increase the confidence levels of their interns, then they have given them something as valuable as the knowledge obtained on internships. They have given them one of the secrets of a successful career.

DEVELOPING AND EXERCISING SUPERVISORY SKILLS

Interns need supervision, and taking on interns offers a supervisory opportunity to professionals in the hosting organization.

Because many interns do not work full time, are not permanent employees, and because they are often not paid and are not critical members of professional teams within organizations, supervisory responsibility for them tends to be somewhat less intense and less demanding than it might be otherwise with full-time entry-level employees. This situation is conducive for new or aspiring supervisors to utilize interns as a means of developing real supervisory experience. Many of the same situations and issues come up over the course of an internship that come up with probationary employees. For one, there is the need to communicate with interns so that they are linked to the chain of command and understand their roles within the organization. Also, there are training requirements for interns, as well as evaluations of their performances and perhaps the occasional requests for time off due to a variety of reasons. All of these typical supervisory situations may need attention and, at times, negotiation. The process needed to orient interns and train them in new professional environments will necessitate thought and planning. Evaluation procedures will need to be developed. Methods for delivering feedback to interns and for debriefing them as part of the evaluation process will need to be worked out in order to ensure their professional growth. Various personnel issues may also arise and require attention, such as tardiness, dress-code, customer service issues, and others. Two examples of dress-code confusion suffice to demonstrate this. At one site, there was a prohibition against wearing open-toed shoes; the intern experienced some understandable embarrassment when she wore such shoes to work. To the supervisor's credit, she sent the intern on a work-related errand that happened to be near a shoe store, provided her with the money to purchase a pair of shoes. In another, less supportive occasion, the intern—at a highly regarded film company in Los Angeles—came to work wearing sandals, thinking that the "laid-back" California culture, as well as the culture of the film industry, permitted this. That particular day, his supervisor had to send the intern to the company president's office on an errand. While it was an honor for the intern to spend a few moments with the most powerful woman in Hollywood, after he left her office, his supervisor received a personal call from the president instructing him never to send anyone to her office in sandals again. To his credit, the supervisor turned this into a valuable learning experience, pointing out that in the film industry, one dresses to the standard of occupation he or she occupies or aspires to. Good advice for all interns.

All of these learning opportunities require new supervisors to develop strategies and to grow their own managerial skills. Because of the importance and complexity of internship supervision, it is vital to establish a chain of command within organizations with respect to internships. While supervisors are responsible for the growth of interns, more experienced managerial personnel must be present to mentor the supervisors. Once again, this establishes internships as a critical aspect of lifelong learning within learning organizations.

EXPANDING TIME AND OPPORTUNITIES FOR SPECIAL PROJECTS

When businesses assume the responsibility of hosting internships, it often provides opportunities to develop special projects that would otherwise remain unfulfilled. In eras of job shrinkage and corporate downsizing, remaining employees find themselves responsible for more and more of the work required to keep a business entity successful; this leaves precious little energy or time for new ideas to be developed or for new opportunities to be explored. Yet the ideas and opportunities do not disappear in such times. Well-qualified interns permit a thinning out of work responsibilities and an expansion of work capability, without creating prohibitive effects on the corporate bottom line. One internship site we interviewed, a book publisher, stated emphatically that hosting an intern allowed them to take three vitally important projects "off the back burner" and complete them during the three months the intern was present. "We are a more profitable company now than we were when the intern arrived," was how the supervisor put it [6].

Because of the additional flexibility interns provide to the organizations that host them, there are several possibilities for structuring special projects. Supervisors may be aware of projects that could be done if there were sufficient time in which to do them. In this case, the goal would be to train interns to do as many of the day-to-day tasks within their department as possible in order to free up another person to pursue the project. Alternately, there may be a special project wherein the interns are the primary motivators. This might result because the interns brought up the idea or because they are in a better position (more time, more recent, up-to-date skills, etc.) to pursue the special project. Or perhaps it is simply easier to train interns for the tasks of special projects than to have them be responsible for the day-to-day work flow. In fact, interns can be chosen specifically because they have a special expertise that prepares them for a particular project.

With certain organizations, special projects are part of their community service. As such, they are valuable to the corporate reputation, if not to the corporate bottom line; but they are valuable nonetheless. Interns, for all the reasons previously stated, contribute time and energy for pursuing these public-relations opportunities.

Potential internship sites would do well to consider developing special projects that can provide goals for even limited internships. Moreover, they might not have the same pressures as a required project. They can galvanize and focus interns as well as provide real and valuable experience.

PROCURING EXTRA HELP

Closely related to the benefits of using interns for special projects is the recognition of them as extra help for organizations. An intern is another person in a department or in an organization. Because interns are usually closer to the end of their academic preparation than to the beginning, they have already received training in their field of study. After experiencing the on-the-job training provided at an internship site, they can usually be assigned the tasks of entry-level employees. These tasks become a significant part of their orientation to the professional environment. In fact, this is the model for internships that we consistently use and just as consistently advocate. In the case of Worcester Memorial Hospital, interns to the Training and Education Department are asked to make copies of videotapes, label those tapes, and keep the collection of tapes organized. As a result, they also become familiar with the training products that the department has developed by watching what they are asked to copy [7]. Tasks and responsibilities can build as interns prove what they can accomplish, with the need for supervision decreasing over time. Often, internships facilitate the orientation process by having interns spend a few hours to a few days with various members of the organization observing what they do and how they do it. This process of shadowing others affords interns an opportunity to develop a feel for the processes, projects, and personalities involved in the new work situation before becoming responsible for their own contributions to the organization.

While interns are extra help in host organizations, there must be a balance between the need of the organization for that extra help and their commitment to provide interns with learning experiences. If an organization is pressed to the point of needing another employee, it would be unwise to think that interns could fulfill that need. Nor would it be fair to the interns who may not be getting paid for their experiences. In the end, even considering all the benefits to the host organizations, interns are quasi-employees who engage in internships primarily to further their professional education. If there is little-to-no time or opportunity for mentoring the interns, a corporation would be advised not to host them.

ENGAGING IN PREEMPLOYMENT SCREENING

Internships serve as an excellent bridge between academic studies and professional work. In challenging economic times, they are an essential mechanism for gaining access to paying professional opportunities. Internships and other forms of experiential learning allow students to test what they have learned in school, obtain exposure to realistic work environments, and gain professional experience, technical skills, and a basic understanding of professional behavior, thereby screening potential sites for future employment. Internships also provide an opportunity for developing portfolio material that allows students to come away with tangible examples of what they are capable of doing. Through the internship process, many students are able to find mentors to whom they can turn for advice, model themselves after, and network into their burgeoning professional community of practice. Internships provide insight that allows students to examine and become consciously aware of the professional processes that are needed to start and sustain a professional career, resulting in a symbiotic energy that has been described as follows:

> The experiential approach [provided in internships] is a powerful motivator for learning because it is positive and meaningful and real. The learning environment is success-oriented rather than competitive. It offers opportunities for real-life problem solving in which feedback is uncontrived and immediate, and in which results are real-life physical and emotional consequences. Because the learners participate in the design, the

> implementation and the management of their own learning, they are invested in the goal, hence internally motivated [8, pp. 1-3].

This becomes, in effect, an ideal realization of Aristotle's ideas concerning *praxis*; through experience, interns come to realize the virtues that they have come to appreciate in their communities of practice and that these constitute a worthwhile way of professional life.

In addition, this statement more than adequately describes the social aspects of communal learning described earlier. The orientation toward success, the participatory nature of designing internships, and the inculcation of principles common to communities of practice all contribute to narrowing Vygotsky's zone of proximal development.

It is not unusual for interns to be hired for freelance, part-time or full-time work by their sites after completion of their internship. When this happens it is a mutually beneficial result of a successful internship. Good employees who assimilate into the corporate culture and have skills required by their host organization are often difficult to find. Interviewing potential employees to figure out whether they will work out is also an inexact science. Trying out potential employees for a probationary period, often up to six months or more, and then determining that they will not work out, is time and money wasted. If interns can be hired for a position following their internships, the probationary period is already over for the organization and its new employee. The employer knows the qualities and skills of the intern. The new employee is already oriented, trained, and ready to contribute professionally from the first day of employment.

One organization we examined had four interns when they realized they were in a position to hire an additional person. They were in the enviable position of being able to seriously evaluate the potential of each intern to fill the position. While the organization could have conducted a traditional employee search, their experience with the interns they knew and had worked with over several months provided an accurate estimate of how each might fit into their professional mission.

Consequently, internships provide excellent opportunities for students to prescreen employment options and for organizations to prescreen potential employees. The social milieu in which internships operate creates important learning opportunities for all involved, permitting both intern and host the ability to determine that necessary fit between the needs of the individual and the organization.

EXPOSURE TO PROFESSIONS

Students choose professions for many reasons, but often it is not until they are exposed to the day-to-day routine of those professions that they can predict whether or not they will enjoy the profession and be suited for success in it. For example, studying criminal justice in the classroom can be very different than dealing with the real situations that police officers face on a daily basis. Stories wherein students study a field for a number of years in college only to abandon it because the realities of the job were not what they expected are, unfortunately, common. Internships can help to alleviate this sort of misfortune because they provide opportunities for students to be exposed to the professional rigors of their discipline at relatively low risk—to the student or to the host site. Accordingly, internships as preprofessional experiences serve as another important aspect of the viable transition between academic and professional environments. Early in their academic careers, if students are not certain regarding their choice of a course of study, they can engage in a series of "shadowing" experiences, whereby they observe a profession first-hand and on-site. Similarly, they might choose to engage in an early internship in the field in which they are potentially interested. At times, a short internship will awaken a student's passions. We have seen students who, after completing such an internship take their academic studies much more seriously because the internship allowed them to see the relationship between what they were studying (*episteme*) and the essential knowledge (*phronesis* and *techne)* for professional performance. Suddenly, academics become real and the relationship between them and successful careers obvious. The process of contemplating, finding, and experiencing an internship can be invaluable to students' career preparation.

Serow reports a similar strategy and its success at Southeast Missouri University in a program that was designed to promote retention in the criminal justice major [9, pp. 50-53]. The program identified students with poor writing skills and paired them with professionals at a professional site where the students could observe firsthand the importance of strong writing skills to the criminal justice profession. The result was a demonstrably positive impact on the students, who, as a consequence of this exposure to professional expectations, understood the importance of written communication and recommitted themselves to mastering it.

INTERNSHIPS AS EXPERIENCE

Many employers will not hire persons who do not have direct experience in the position they are seeking to fill. Many prospective employees, especially those who are fresh from an academic environment, cannot get experience because no one will hire them without experience. Internships can provide a way out of this dilemma because they furnish professional experience. Unpaid internships are particularly attractive to organizations that are concerned about personnel expense, because they receive low-cost or no-cost labor in exchange for providing the intern with professional-level experience that will support them in making the necessary transition to their first paying position in their new profession. Internships provide that missing link between academic environments and professions: experience. However, it needs to be appropriate experience—that which provides professional responsibilities and activities combined with ongoing learning opportunities. That combination promotes in student preprofessionals the sort of confidence in their abilities required to successfully compete for their first fully professional position. Rosmann supports this in describing a program for social-science majors at the University of Virginia: "Interns rate themselves as significantly more fulfilled, active, worthwhile, and possessing a more broadened outlook on life than students who have not participated in the program" [10].

LIFELONG LEARNING

The sort of experiential learning that internships can provide creates a foundation for a variety of lifelong learning opportunities. Hornbeck supports this observation: "It does not take a learning theorist to conclude that one of the ways we learn is by doing" [11, pp. 17-18]. Williams concurs:

> Twelve studies of field education are reviewed here. . . . Field education does promote the development of young people and this development is reflected in measures of achievement, self-concept, career maturity, values, and attitudes [12, p. 130].

While we would certainly not disagree with either of these sentiments, one of our theses in this book is to better understand, through learning theories as well as inquiries into practical matters, how internships provide for valuable learning experiences.

With regard to the practical, corporations often have equipment that educational institutions cannot afford and therefore are able to provide or enhance specialized skills education for interns. Similarly, undergraduate degree programs, in particular, often cannot offer specific academic courses in every subject area in which students are interested or even, on occasions, in every area they need. Such programs provide a foundation for their students and, it is hoped, a commitment to and understanding of the importance of lifelong learning. But as Serow points out, "By their very nature, internships, practica, service-learning, and other forms of experiential education [enable] . . . programs [to] be adapted to the interests [and needs] of students" [9, p. 3].

In addition to providing opportunities for specialized skills education, internships also provide the opportunity to see how the parts of an organization fit together to form a functioning whole. They allow interns to observe professional working relationships in order to begin learning the complex fundamentals of corporate politics. Developing successful relationships with co-workers, supervisors, and any of the other constituencies to which interns are exposed is an important aspect of becoming a competent professional.

We have found that learning how to work with clients has often been a major educational development for students, particularly in the field of graphic design. Graphics interns, for instance, are frequently surprised at the client's power to determine the creative direction of a graphic-design piece. The intern's prior academic experience has mostly been to create artwork that satisfies the demands of a professor and the pedagogical requirements of the course in which it was designed. Consequently, in some interns' minds, the graphic-design professionals are the ones who have studied the discipline and who have developed the appropriate expertise upon which their design opinions are founded and to which other (perhaps uninformed) opinions should defer. Learning that this is not the way the real world works is a large step toward becoming a competent professional. Clients who hire the design firm expect to have an important say in final design decisions, and it is important for interns to learn the skills necessary to tactfully persuade clients that the design decisions of the professional are in fact the best decisions. Even so, any professional graphic designer, photographer, corporate video or film producer, technical writer, and so on has had many experiences in which clients made bad decisions and stuck with them. That is the nature of these industries. Interns can begin to ensure that these experiences are rare in their professional careers by developing skills that inculcate trust between client and artist. Witnessing a seasoned professional manipulate the client's idea while massaging the client's ego in just such a way so as to preserve the design integrity of the work is one of the values of internships.

Another challenge to client relationships that interns need to learn and adapt to has to do with different senses of time. Again, from our experience with seasoned professionals in a wide range of communications industries, time and again we have heard stories of clients who want a quick turnaround on design work, but who themselves do not provide equally quick feedback on sample designs. As a result, projects lag, budgets fester, and overhead expenses build. These issues are particularly threatening to smaller companies. Interns gain valuable experience witnessing how professionals overcome such obstacles, including learning how to develop productive two-way communication strategies between client and professional.

Recently, one of our interns was surprised to learn of the power that the marketing department had to dictate priorities in the training and development department in which he was interning. At first, this did not appear to make sense to him. It was not until the important connections between training in the use of products and marketing strategies was made clear to him that he finally understood. In this particular situation, the company was competing in an area where they had decided to use the training provided with complex electronic equipment as a distinguishing feature of what they were offering, a difference that they hoped would make their own products more competitive.

In a completely different environment, another intern complained to her supervisor about having to give tours to school groups at a museum because, as a graphic design student, that was not what she had spent four years in college and considerable money learning how to do. Rather than agree with her, the supervisor was able to carefully explain the reasons behind giving tours, despite the fact that this appeared to her to be a mundane and uninteresting task. The supervisor pointed out that by carefully observing what customers relate to and comment on provides excellent research for developing design ideas that would successfully promote the museum. Taking this advice to heart, the intern approached being a tour guide with renewed enthusiasm and later admitted that her knowledge of the museum's holdings, as well as its customers, enriched her understanding of how to best apply her professional design skills on subsequent assignments.

At times, the most poignant lessons interns learn have to do with the ongoing development of a relationship between the intern and supervisor. As all successful professionals know, attaining success involves much more than simply applying skills to known situations. Being a lifelong learner requires applying skills to unknown situations, which produce the results that are new, fresh, different, and exciting.

This is the lesson that helps interns learn how their chosen field operates in a professional manner within the context of the organization. Interns not only learn by doing but can learn from observing, questioning, and studying other professionals who are doing the job they wish to pursue. While such learning experiences will undoubtedly be rich, one of their most important aspects is developing an understanding of the ever-evolving relationship between professionals, their supervisors, and their clients. Schon supports this conclusion by suggesting that "effective problem solving relies less on formal education and more on improvisation learned in practice" [13].

PORTFOLIOS AS PROOF OF QUALIFICATIONS

Internships provide professional experience to interns, who are often able to develop tangible examples of what they accomplished during their internships. These examples become the interns' professional portfolios and may take the form of written reports, advertising layouts, kitchen designs, or any other tangible proof of the interns' accomplishments. As long as issues of corporate confidentiality and proprietary information are addressed, interns can use these pieces as evidence of their professional capabilities.

Interns should always keep in mind the possibility of their projects being represented in a portfolio that would allow prospective employers to directly examine their level of work. As a result, they should collect material for such purposes during their internship, with permission of the host site, of course.

Some interns are reluctant to use material that they did not solely create themselves, but there are viable ways to acknowledge teamwork and the intern's individual contributions to a piece of work. As opposed to interns' academic experiences, real business projects are almost always team driven, blending the specialized skills of individuals in such ways that the final product is greater than the sum of its parts. Emphasizing both individual contributions and successful teamwork through a portfolio of professional work is a highly competitive strategy for students seeking their first professional position following an internship and graduation.

In developing their portfolios, interns should always keep in mind the necessity of explaining the criteria they used for selecting the works displayed. Each piece must be a substantive contribution to support the interns' knowledge and abilities, while also depicting the potential the intern has for future development as a successful professional. Moreover, interns need to realize that they will not have a one-size-fits-all portfolio. Different sample works can be used for different interviews in order to custom design the portfolio for each job application. Doing so demonstrates forethought on the part of the job applicants, research about the field into which they plan to enter, and knowledge of the specific position for which they are applying. Tightly matching a portfolio to the expectations published about a job is an important skill for interns to learn.

Perhaps even more importantly, portfolio development skills can and should be introduced into the professional courses that precede internships. In this way, students learn the necessity of proving their competencies with artifacts from individual and group projects. This rightly creates a professional culture within the academic environment of certain disciplines.

FINDING A MENTOR FOR INTERNSHIP EXPERIENCES

A mentor is someone who is trustworthy and respectable—an accomplished professional who can guide interns by giving them advice, tutoring, or coaching. A mentor can help develop an aspiring professional in many ways, such as becoming a role model. By discovering and understanding the foundations of the mentor's success, interns may be able to enhance their career preparation and advancement. They may also be able to observe and learn from the methods and techniques their mentor uses to deal with professional relationships and the inevitable challenges that arise in the work environment. Similarly, the mentor could also model how to stay current in one's field through continued professional development, whether it be through attending conferences and workshops, reading a steady stream of books and journals, or engaging in additional training.

However internship supervisors are not always the most likely choice for mentors. Even though they probably have the level of expertise from which interns can learn, sometimes the role of supervisor can get in the way of actually asking the supervisor for advice. For example, if the intern needs to ask for several hours off on a coming afternoon and would like to get some advice on how best to present that request, asking the supervisor for such advice (since it is the supervisor who would grant the request) is illogical. Nonetheless, in reality most supervisors do end up being a de facto mentor to most interns.

In addition to the coaching and professional modeling mentors provide, they can also assist interns beyond their internships by providing access to their professional network. Making connections with other people in the field at other companies or at other departments in the same company can be extremely advantageous when it comes time to look for a paying position.

NETWORKING AFTER INTERNSHIPS

Networking is the utilization of a professional support system that develops by knowing other people in the field. The members of one's network should be easy to call and ask for professional advice on a wide variety of issues. If one can develop a network and keep in regular contact with the people in it, he or she is provided with a collection of unofficial friendly consultants who can give their perspectives on a situation or issue. Moreover, networking can go beyond the boundaries of other members in the same profession. Ideally, students, while on internship, will begin to form professional networks that will benefit their growth and development throughout their careers. This is perhaps the most important of all the valuable learning opportunities in which students engage while participating in internships designed to be professional experiences.

SUMMARY

The benefits to corporations of hosting interns are many and various. At the core of internship experiences are people who can mentor and influence young, eager, would-be professionals. In exchange for this mentoring, host organizations are able to engage in new projects, expand their workforce without expanding their bottom line, and, perhaps most importantly, contribute to the ongoing growth and development of their professions. These benefits have accrued to organizations that have engaged in internships for centuries and clearly will extend well into the twenty-first century as an important facet of successful learning organizations. Professional experiences, the basis of valuable internships, create learning experiences that will form the foundation for future growth and development. They provide a milieu that supports and demonstrates the social aspects of learning within a profession. They inculcate the important, and perhaps second-nature knowledge of Aristotle's philosophy as to what constitutes a successful person—the interaction of *episteme, phronesis,* and *praxis.*

REFERENCES

1. E. Kaplan, Commercial Ware, Inc., Natick, MA [personal interview], 2002.
2. A. Cunningham, Tufts University School of Veterinary Medicine, North Grafton, MA [personal interview], 2002.
3. E. U. Howell, Turner Sports Marketing, Atlanta, GA [personal interview], 1998.
4. L. S. Vygotsky, *Mind and Society.* Cambridge: Cambridge University Press, 1978.
5. W. Ramsey, *Combining Service and Learning: A Resource Book for Community Public Service, Vol. II,* J. Kendall (ed.). New York: Jossey-Bass, 1974.
6. R. Brown, Genzyme Corporation, Framingham, MA [personal interview], 1999.
7. L. K. Lee, Norwalk Hospital, Norwalk, CT [personal interview], 2002.
8. A nation at risk: Another view, *Experiential Education, 9*:2, March-April, 1984. (A joint statement of the Association for Experiential Education and the Council for Adult and Experiential Learning.)
9. R. C. Serow, *The Program Evaluation Handbook,* Needham Heights, MA: Simon and Schuster Custom Publications, 1998.

10. M. R. Rosmann, *Undergraduate Internships for Social Science Majors: Development and Longitudinal Evaluation of a Model Program.* ERIC #161812-5001289, p. 1, March 1978.
11. D. W. Hornbeck, "Not the school alone," *Synergist. National Center for Service Learning, ACTION, 10*: 2, 1981.
12. R. Williams, "The voice of volunteers," in *The Impact of Field Education on Student Development: Research Findings*. Sharon, MA: The Korda Project, 1980.
13. D. Schon, *The Reflective Practitioner: How Professionals Think in Action*. New York: Basic Books, frontispiece author's note, 1983.

CHAPTER 4

Administrative Responsibilities for Academic Institutions

> One of the ways we complement the academic institution when we host interns is to assign one staff member to be an intern "mentor." This should be someone who does a job similar to what the student is studying and can help assign projects, or answer questions and guide the students during the experience. The mentor can be in addition to the on-site supervisor.
>
> *Dawn Haley*
> *Fablevision*

Colleges and universities may choose to manage internships in a variety of ways. This chapter reviews the benefits and challenges of various approaches to administrative responsibilities for academic institutions sponsoring internship programs as part of their curricula. It also describes experiences based on the authors' involvement with the internship program in their department.

FULL-TIME VERSUS PART-TIME INTERNSHIPS

Full-time internships present colleges and their students with certain advantages. For one, no other internship arrangement approximates entry-level work experience as closely. The companies and organizations with which we have partnered for over two decades tell us repeatedly that they give preference to our interns because of their professional readiness and because they will gain a full-time, probationary employee for almost four months. The advantage to the college or university providing interns to companies is a strongly developed sense of responsibility, especially when it is based on a long-standing relationship between the academic institution and the host internship site. These organizations can count on, and even come to rely on, the full-time interns such an institution provides.

Students also reap the benefits of full-time internships. One of the biggest hurdles college graduates are encountering in the early twenty-first century is obtaining their first professional position following graduation. Job placement for college graduates currently appears to be as challenging as at any time in the past 30 years. Full-time internships provide students with several months of real-world professional experience, which they can use to gain an advantage over their competition. It is this advantage, we believe, that has allowed our academic department to maintain a 91% placement rate for our graduates into their professions within 6 months of graduation over the past 20 years.

Despite the fact that, as internship directors, we are fundamentally supportive of full-time internships, there are some disadvantages that need mentioning. The most important of these is that a full-time, semester-long internship takes an enormous portion out of a student's college academic career, in terms of both time and academic credits (in our department's case, 12 credits out of a total 120 credits required for graduation). Our particular internship is the capstone graduation requirement for our students; it occurs in their senior year after all other academic requirements have been met. This means that students must be particularly industrious (and at times unusually mature) in planning out their academic program in order to be ready for a full-time internship in three and a half years. Approximately 35% of our students do not attain that goal and spend a fifth year at the college readying themselves for the internship [1]. This adds financial costs to their education that they (and perhaps their parents) might not have originally planned for.

Full-time internships also present an additional financial burden to many students, especially those who have worked throughout their academic career to help fund their education or support themselves. A 40-hour per week internship plus commuting time cuts severely into the available hours for part-time paying work. Schedules must often be reworked, requiring an understanding and flexible employer. Some students find part-time work to be impossible during their internship and, consequently, must spend the years prior to internship saving enough money to see themselves through the experience. Another potential expense occurs when the internship is at a location far from the college or university. Many of our internships are located throughout the country and, increasingly, internationally. Students who desire such an internship must plan for the living expenses associated with it.

The final disadvantage to full-time internships has to do with a special category of students who are more frequently attending colleges and universities across the country—the mature and returning student. Students who have family and professional obligations, along with their academic careers, find taking time for a full-time internship to be particularly challenging. Nonetheless, when the college, student, employer, and host organization are flexible, workable arrangements can be discovered that will permit such students to engage in a successful internship. Despite the challenges, we rarely encounter a situation in which the internship is impossible. All students, including mature and returning ones, must be made aware of the requirements associated with full-time internships *upon matriculation.* That provides such students with ample time to plan, as well as ample reason to reconsider whether or not the program is best suited for them.

Part-time internships basically provide students with advantages associated with the disadvantages of full-time internships. They require less time out of the academic career of the student; in fact, many part-time internships can be effectively scheduled into the ongoing academic semesters, occurring at times that do not conflict with class schedules. As such, they are less likely to impede the completion of academic requirements for graduation. Additionally, since part-time internships generally consume 10 to 20 hours per week, they pose less of a financial threat to students who also work part-time to support themselves.

Part-time internships, by their very nature, preclude obtaining an internship a great distance from the college or university. Because such internships generally occur during a semester rather than in place of it, students do not incur additional living expenses as a result, though they may incur some additional commuting expense. Moreover, part-time internships are particularly well suited for mature and returning students who have other significant responsibilities.

But there are, we believe, significant disadvantages to part-time internships. The most important is that they do not provide the consistent professional experience full-time internships do. Hosts repeatedly report that the learning experience is vastly different and inferior for part-time internships compared with full-time internships. They note that part-time interns spend a significant amount of time relearning and repeating entry-level experiences as a result of the limited amount of time spent on the internship; whereas full-time interns build consistently upon those experiences, developing professional competence as a result. Moreover, hosts report that it is very difficult to assign part-time interns a bona fide project, as they would an entry-level employee, because most companies and organizations do not have the luxury of allowing a project to languish during the intern's absence.

Additionally, full-time interns develop deeper and more meaningful professional relationships with their colleagues on the job than do part-time interns. Internship supervisors often become important mentors in the early career development of students and remain so, even after the internship has been completed and the student has graduated. Full-time internships provide ample time for such mentoring relationships to develop fully.

For these reasons, we believe that full-time internships are significantly more successful for students, host sites, and colleges than part-time internships, and we recommend that any institution considering developing an internship program strongly consider the full-time option.

FOR-CREDIT INTERNSHIPS VERSUS FOR-PAY INTERNSHIPS

Academic institutions that are in the process of developing internship programs must also consider whether they will be for credit or for pay. Here, too, there are advantages and disadvantages to each approach.

For-credit internships permit the colleges and universities granting such credit to retain overall responsibility for the internship. That is an enormous advantage to the academic institution in that it retains the final say in how internships are designed and managed. In addition, for-credit internships stress the academic nature of the preprofessional learning experiences. This strikes us as appropriate and as a result has been one of the underlying themes of this book.

Interestingly, it has also been our experience that interns who are not paid are given more professional responsibilities than those who are paid. In asking hosts about this apparent anomaly, their response has been consistent. Again and again, they point out that unpaid interns present no financial risk to the host organization. As a result, management at these organizations is often more willing to permit the intern to take on responsibilities they would not grant to an intern whose work appears on the bottom line. Without the financial risk, host organizations consistently appear more willing to undertake professional risks that lead to more rewarding learning experiences for the interns.

For-credit internships involve fewer disadvantages. They include ensuring that the internship is a viable component of the curriculum and the financial burden to students who participate in unpaid internships. The first is not really a disadvantage, but rather a challenge to program design and development. For example, in academic departments such as ours that require a capstone full-time semester-long internship, the curriculum is essentially designed in such a way that everything prior to internship prepares for internship. And as has been previously mentioned, the financial burdens to students can be lessened or eliminated entirely by planning from the point of entering college up to the date an internship begins.

For-pay internships have distinct and identifiable advantages as well, but they are significantly different from for-credit internships. Obviously, paying internships lessen the financial burdens placed upon student interns. A paying internship also replicates the professional environment in which employees are paid for the work they do. This is an important characteristic of the paying internship, and it is significantly different from for-credit internships that place the emphasis on the learning or academic experience. Paying interns for the work they do instills a logical connection between professional endeavors and compensation that, oddly, at times seems to be missing, even among students who have had part-time jobs for years.

In our experience, however, there are important disadvantages to for-pay internships. Among these is the quality of work that seems to be associated with such internships. As mentioned above, most organizations we have worked with provide a better professional experience to interns they do not have to pay. Paid interns are more frequently relegated to the least important tasks available—copying, filing, running errands. This is so common in our experience that one of the hallmarks of our for-credit internships is that they *must* be founded upon professional work experience rather than menial tasks. As a result, we have regularly had interns earn their way into significant professional experiences that are more often associated with entry-level employment than with internships.

For these reasons, it is our recommendation that academic institutions considering the development of internship programs explore the advantages of for-credit, nonpaying internships for their students. The academic emphasis, the focus on learning, and the opportunity to perform real professional work greatly outweigh the ephemeral connections that can be made between performance and a (meager) salary.

In addressing what might seem an obvious omission, is it possible for internships to be both for pay and for credit? To our knowledge, there is no universal restriction against this, and some academic institutions do, in fact, engage in such internships. It is our belief and experience, however, that such internships combine the disadvantages of both types without reaping the rewards. Students have difficulty serving the two masters of academic institution and employer. Responsibility for the internship, though theoretically shared, is less clear than under either arrangement separately. And it is unclear at the end of the internship whether or not the student has had a learning experience or a professional experience. We would therefore advise against attempts to combine for-pay and for-credit internships, but if there is one aspect of this book that deserves further and more rigorous study, it would be this combination.

If academic institutions adopt for-credit internships, the final consideration is to ensure that they meet national Carnegie requirements. The full-time, semester-long internships our department requires receive 12 academic credits (in the semester system). As such, they require a minimum of 37.5 hours of professional work per week to meet the Carnegie standard. As part of the academic expectations, students also keep a journal of their activities and reflections and fulfill several academic assignments that are appropriate to preprofessional study. These include revising their résumés to include the internship experience and applying for their first professional position, under the tutelage of their professional internship supervisor and their academic internship supervisor. They also research and complete a final paper that analyzes the company for which they have interned. Their analysis focuses on the history of the company, its corporate culture, its stability, and its outlooks for the future. Such a paper becomes an important component of students' portfolios in the event they apply to graduate school, because many graduate programs in communications-related disciplines focus—appropriately—on theoretical inquiry into professional practice. A final paper that carefully analyzes the internship experience within a particular corporate culture prepares students well for that type of academic enterprise.

CAPSTONE INTERNSHIPS VERSUS INTERMEDIARY INTERNSHIPS

There are also options as to when internships can and should occur. Many colleges and universities use the internship as a capstone experience, a way of assessing the outcomes of an academic program in terms of preparing students for professions after graduation. Other institutions permit and encourage students to engage in internships at virtually any point after their first year of study. Here, too, there are advantages and disadvantages to each approach.

In professional programs especially, students seem to need to have completed their academic preparation in order to successfully engage in an internship that requires them to perform as professionals in their field. Earlier, quasi-internship experiences might be permitted, but they tend to be more of the job-shadowing type of experience rather than full-fledged professional experiences. While these experiences can impress upon students a certain verisimilitude with regard to the career paths they have chosen, they are still, at best, likenesses of professional experiences and not the experience itself. In nonprofessional academic programs, such a distinction is probably not as consequential, and therefore, intermediary internships would more than likely work as well as capstone internships, provided that students had reached an appropriate maturity to engage in the internships and reap their benefits fully.

Given our experience, the successful internship program our department has had for over 25 years, and weighing the advantages and disadvantages of a variety of internship designs, we highly recommend full-time, semester-long, credit-granting internships that are required as the students' capstone academic experience immediately prior to graduation as a transitional step to the professional world.

PREPARING STUDENTS FOR SUCCESSFUL INTERNSHIPS

Preparing students for a full-time, semester-long, credit-granting internship is in itself a significant undertaking that should take place the semester immediately prior to the internship. We have found that such preparation best falls into the following categories:

- Internship preparation seminars
- Résumés, letters of application, personal professional statements
- Portfolios and portfolio defenses

With the internship being viewed as an academic experience, we schedule four 90-minute seminars early in the semester prior to internship. The first seminar covers the qualifications students must meet in order to be considered for placement, as well as the expectations for students while they are engaged in the internship. The second seminar covers the design and writing of résumés, letters of application, and personal professional statements, all of which become part of the students' application packages, as well as part of their professional portfolios. The third seminar examines professional portfolios and the required portfolio defense that we expect every student to complete successfully. The final seminar is for questions and answers that have arisen as a result of the first three, as well as a discussion of the expectations students will have to meet while on internship.

If the internship is to serve as a student's capstone academic experience, then all other academic requirements must be met prior to engaging in the internship. In our first seminar we explain that this includes the completion of all academic requirements for the students' major, all college-wide academic requirements, and a grade point average that meets predetermined requirements. Our grade-point requirement is in three tiers, limited to the students' performance in courses within their major, depending upon the type of internship they desire: 2.5 on a 4.0 scale to qualify for the internship in general; 3.0 to qualify for internships outside a day's commute from the college; and 3.3 for international internships. Our rationale for these requirements is that we are in a preprofessional department, and it is our assumption that students who perform better in their preprofessional major courses will require less immediate supervision from their academic internship directors.

We have found that the grade-point average in students' preprofessional courses is a reasonably accurate predictor of their success while on internship.

The first seminar also reviews the expectations placed upon students during the internship qualification process. These include attendance at all preparatory seminars, a successful defense of the professional portfolio before a faculty committee, and a successful exit interview with the internship director.

The second seminar is devoted to the basic expectations centered around applying for a professional position. These include résumé design, writing application letters, and developing a personal professional statement. Numerous excellent resources exist for each of these, and we are somewhat flexible in allowing students to design materials that meet their needs as well as satisfy the expectations of their profession. Several sample résumés are included in the Appendix to demonstrate the differences in designing a résumé for entry into various professions.

Letters of application and personal professional statements are, as would be expected, highly individualistic, designed to present the applicant as a distinct individual to the potential host organization. A sample personal professional statement is also included in the Appendix.

The third seminar is devoted to explaining professional portfolio development and preparing students for defending their portfolios before a faculty committee. In actuality, this preparation begins during the students' summer orientation session prior to their freshman year in our department, at which we communicate that every assignment in our department's courses should be treated as professional in nature, and that the very best of these assignments will later compose their professional portfolio, which they must defend in order to qualify for their senior internship. It is a message that gets repeated consistently throughout their academic career.

Pedagogically, the disciplines of communications and media can be thought of as applied liberal arts, similar to thinking of engineering as applied science. As such, these disciplines fit well into Aristotle's concepts of *techne* and *praxis*. Portfolios provide college faculty, college administrators, and corporate management with proof of a prospective intern's readiness for the professional world. That proof is in the form of artifacts created by the students. Therefore portfolio development should be a continuous process throughout students' academic careers. And their individual portfolios should evolve as their expertise and interests do.

Portfolios are individualistic, as is to be expected. They contain only the work that best represents the students' professional capabilities and, depending upon their major, could include writing samples, art and design work, and DVDs containing film or video productions. In keeping with professional expectations, we strongly encourage all students to create an electronic version of their portfolios, which can be cheaply and effectively left with the organizations they apply to.

Several weeks after the conclusion of the preparatory seminars, students schedule a portfolio defense with a faculty committee, which includes the internship director and a faculty member from the student's professional discipline. Because of the nature of our department and its preprofessional emphasis, we have designed these defenses to resemble a shortened version of the defenses for a Masters degree of Fine Arts (MFA). Ours run 30 minutes, during which time students present their work and faculty members critique and question students about it. Ours being an undergraduate program, the emphasis is as much on support, ongoing learning, and professional development as it is on defense. Nonetheless, students approach the defense as being the single most important event of their academic careers.

If any unresolved issues remain after the first 3 seminars are completed, they are dealt with at the fourth and final seminar, along with explaining what the college will expect of interns while they are on their internships. Most often, students have questions regarding qualifications and how internship placement decisions are made. But other questions can involve a range of interests, from the corporate culture into which the intern will be placed to dress codes within that culture, aspects of professional demeanor, required assignments, and so forth.

FACULTY INVOLVEMENT AS INTERNSHIP SUPERVISORS

There are many ways to supervise an intern's performance. Some institutions utilize a separate office of internships and provide supervision by staff members from it. Other institutions engage faculty members from the interns' academic departments.

As has been the case with other aspects of internship design, how a college or university structures internship academic supervision also has a variety of advantages and disadvantages.

Removing internship academic supervision from the academic departments in which students have been educated has certain advantages. For one, it does not take faculty time away from other professorial activities—teaching, research, or service. Another advantage is that in many, perhaps most, cases having a staff member from an office of internships supervise is less expensive than having a faculty member do it. But there are disadvantages to this arrangement as well: the most serious is that staff members in a separate office of internships must to a certain degree master all the disciplines of a college or university in order to provide more than superficial and rudimentary supervision. In our analysis of these arrangements, supervision tends to devolve into ensuring that deadlines are met, appropriate forms are completed, and interns are progressing appropriately toward the completion of their internship. Supervision by staff members rarely seems to engage interns in the sort of professional-to-professional interaction that faculty-supervised internships do.

Having faculty supervise internships provides all the advantages that staff-supervised internships do not, but adds certain significant challenges as well. Faculty from students' academic departments can just as easily determine that interns are completing the minutiae of the internships as well as internship office staff members can, but they can also engage both interns and their on-site professional supervisors in ways that staff members rarely can—from a perspective of shared knowledge about the discipline. It is for this reason that we recommend that faculty supervise internships.

But having faculty perform as supervisors also creates challenges. The most significant of these concerns faculty teaching load and reduced time for academic administrative responsibilities. In over 25 years of experience, we have come to the conclusion that supervising between 6 and 9 interns in a full-time internship that corresponds to a semester in length is the equivalent of one 3-credit course. The more interns an academic department has, the more faculty supervisors it needs; and the more faculty who are supervising interns, consequently, creates a need for other faculty to teach the courses that supervisors would have been teaching. Some academic departments fill this need with part-time faculty, and this seems an appropriate albeit costly solution.

MAINTAINING RELATIONSHIPS WITH INTERNSHIP HOST SITES

Maintaining good long-term relationships with host sites is a key to successful internship programs. Such relationships are the result of carefully matching interns to host sites and balancing the expectations of academic institutions with those of the host organizations.

Matching interns and internship host sites is a process that includes exploring students' wishes for their internship, certifying their qualifications based upon the presentation and defense of their professional portfolios, and determining the needs of willing host organizations. Our internships are competitive. Students are told this as part of their summer orientation prior to freshman year, and they are aware that when they become seniors they will be competing with classmates for the best internships. But as internship directors, our fundamental desire is that every student participate in a successful, rewarding professional internship that will provide the transitional step into their careers. As a result, we pay close attention to matching students' desires and abilities with host-site expectations.

Our fundamental presupposition is that every host organization we partner with will provide professional experience that corresponds to that of an entry-level position in their company. Beyond that, we assess the professional rigor that each site provides to and expects of its interns. We do this to ensure that students' abilities are well-suited to a site's expectations. There are high-profile, high-stress sites that we use only for our most highly qualified students. Other sites provide equally valuable learning experiences for students but in an environment that is less demanding. These are appropriate placements for students who might not yet be quite ready to undertake the full responsibilities of professional work within their field. As has been mentioned previously, one of the principles of viewing internships as learning experiences is that students of all levels be mentored in ways that encourage professional growth. Carefully matching interns with host sites accomplishes this and, as a result, helps to build long-term successful relationships between academic institutions and corporate enterprises.

PLACING STUDENTS AT INTERNSHIP HOST SITES

Once students have been certified to qualify for their internship, the final step in the process is to place them in appropriate internships. As part of maintaining good relationships with host sites, we recommend that internship directors actually place students by providing the contact information for an internship that best suits the needs and abilities of the students. We neither encourage nor permit having students find their own internships; although if they are interested in particular sites, discussing that interest becomes one part of the process of deciding what site would be best.

The decisions regarding placement are handled best, we think, in the exit interviews we conduct once the qualification process is complete. Following a successful portfolio defense, students meet with the internship director to discuss interests. At that interview, the director provides students with names and phone numbers of supervisors at the recommended site. We discourage contact by e-mail, despite the prevalence and growing importance of this communication medium, because e-mail is easy to ignore and phone calls are more personal. It has been our experience that students who rely on e-mail contacts require longer periods of time and repeated attempts to obtain a response from a potential host organization. Phone calls are responded to more quickly, and they provide students with an opportunity to demonstrate their professional demeanor as well as to articulate their desires in an internship.

If there appears to be a matching interest between host and potential intern, an application interview is scheduled. During the exit interview with the internship director, tactics for successful interviews are discussed. Many students, certainly the best ones, will often return for follow-up advising immediately prior to their interview.

Once the interview has taken place, we require that students meet again with the internship director for a debriefing session, which explores how well the interview went and whether or not the student was offered an internship. Backup plans are also discussed in case the student does not secure an internship with his or her first choice.

Clearly, not all students excel at the same level. Placing students who have marginal qualifications is a challenge for any internship program, because one must balance the needs of the student with the expectations of the host site, and protect the department's and college's reputation at the same time. This is the primary reason we advocate internship placement, making use of an active role for the internship director in matching student qualifications with site needs. Some sites turn out to be better mentors of students who need additional growth before entering the professional world, while others expect students to be completely ready for that world. At all times, we work closely with the sites that have been chosen for their mentoring characteristics to ensure that here, too, the internship experience is successful for all involved.

CONCLUSION

This chapter represents but one way to design and manage a successful internship program. From our research into the programs at other colleges and universities,[1] we strongly believe it is equal to or exceeds those programs in its thoroughness and effectiveness. Over 25 years of success resulting in several thousand former interns who are now productive professionals within their chosen fields supports our conclusions [2].

REFERENCES

1. Office of Planning, Fitchburg State College, Fitchburg, MA, 2004.
2. Office of Career Placement, Fitchburg State College, Fitchburg, MA, 2004.

[1] Numerous college and university catalogs, Web sites, and academic plan books were collected and analyzed in preparation for the writing of this book.

CHAPTER 5

Administrative Responsibilities for Host Internship Sites

> An internship program is a must for businesses, but only businesses that have the right position or enough work to keep interns busy. Otherwise it's a waste of time for the student. Interns need to be challenged daily. Non-paying internships pay interns in experiences and contacts. You can't place a value on that. It humbles them and teaches them not to base their careers on monetary matters, at least initially. Interns come to understand the relationship between work and reward, and this is not something they can learn out of a book. Properly designed and managed, internships help students get their first job. Many times if there is a great intern, there is a great future employee. Internships can be a great resource pool for entry-level positions. The company knows what interns are capable of as prospective employees before you hire them. You can't always determine that based on the interview process, which is truly a gamble.
>
> *Ellen Wallet*
> *Arnold Worldwide*

Providing professional internships to college students in such a way that the experiences promote learning and inculcate in students knowledge of their discipline as well as their chosen professional community involves many necessary tasks and responsibilities. Similar to much of the rest of what has been presented in this book, these issues can be seen through the eyes of both Aristotle and Vygotsky. Companies that take an active role in providing student internships engage in creating an environment in which students develop the *techne* of their disciplines. As students grow professionally and become fully functioning partners in these disciplines, they begin to evolve their own personal sense of *praxis,* recognizing discipline-based excellence in collegial communities of practice. Both experiences focus Vygotsky's zone of proximal development, as students move through the transition from intern to professional.

Aspects of logistical and affective support, as well as aspects of supervision, nature of duties, length of engagement, and other factors, play important roles in ensuring that the internship is successful for the host site and the intern alike. A supportive community in which the focus is on both occupational and social aspects of learning should be at the core of internship design and administration. What is required of host corporations will vary to some extent based on the intern, the nature of the internships, the resources of the corporation, and the culture of the corporation. However, there are certain minimum logistical and affective foundations that need to be considered before the decision to host is made.

LOGISTICAL SUPPORT

Logistical support includes all aspects of the physical environment in which interns are to work and needs to be evaluated prior to their arrival at the host organization. Some interns need only a modicum of physical support, while others, depending upon the duties the host organization expects of them, will need the basic support of any entry-level employee: a desk, a computer, a phone, and any number of other supportive technologies necessary for a professional to perform effectively. Some of these needs will be resolved by the expectations that host organizations bring to internships, others by the goals that potential interns have for the experience. Most interns expect to reside physically at their site for a certain number of hours each week, but this is not always the case. In situations where a site does not have the facilities to support tasks and projects that interns may be expected to perform, then they may be required to use their own personal facilities for part of the internship experience or the facilities at the college from which they came. While far from an ideal arrangement between host sites and interns, such expectations still allow for the completion of whatever professional objectives the internship is designed to provide, as well as the associated physical work products; although our concerns are that this arrangement diminishes the important social learning aspects of internships—simply because interns in such situations are not present for the entirety of the internship, diminishing the likelihood that they will develop mentoring relationships and the sense of community that are available to interns who are present at their site for the duration of the experience. Despite this, in certain fields, particularly those that might lead to freelancing opportunities later in the intern's career, this arrangement might nonetheless prove adequate in meeting most of the potentials associated with internships. But it requires that interns who undertake such situations have sufficient skills and the ability to work independently.

This situation occurred recently in our experience when an intern wished to engage in an internship that would allow her the opportunity to design and produce graphics and display work for a medieval-themed museum that had clear graphic design needs but virtually no in-house graphic production capabilities. In such a situation, the intern assumes the role of an outside vendor or freelance consultant, and the internship site becomes the client. The intern, necessarily, was a highly motivated, independent, and mature person, ideally suited to the requirements of working productively without constant and present supervision. As a result, this internship proved successful, but had the intern not been matched ideally with this host site, the outcome might not have been as rewarding for both. And even though the internship was deemed successful, certainly the intern's experience of the social aspects of learning within the milieu of the site and that particular discipline was—if not less than—then certainly different from the experience an intern would have had at the museum, provided that she or he was physically present in the museum for the duration of the internship.

While successful internships can be designed in this manner, they require unusual maturity, talent, and skills on the part of the intern. The sponsor and the intern involved in this situation needed to understand the potential challenges and rewards before contracting for the internship. At a minimum, a number of meetings were required between the intern and the sponsor in which projects were planned and parameters and needs covered. During these meetings, socialization to the culture of the site occurred to some extent, so that the intern could effectively provide materials that would be appropriate to the site's needs. And because the actual design and production work would not take place at the site, arrangements for those resources had to be worked out as well. In the end, because of the maturity of the intern and the willing support of the museum, both parties were satisfied with the results. Moreover, the young woman graduated with a body of work that would support her eventual desire to become a freelance graphic artist. Many of the social aspects of learning applied here, but in ways that we might not automatically consider when thinking of the traditional design of internships.

In other internship experiences, interns may be able to do without their own space and utilize existing shared space within the host organization. For instance, we have placed interns in sites that provided space in the company libraries, conference rooms, and even the lunchroom as their primary base within an organization. While this physical arrangement may not be ideal, it is equally true that not all interns must have their own dedicated professional space for the internship to be successful. Nonetheless, environmental needs should be considered and discussed with potential interns beforehand—particularly for those engaged in full-time experiences—so their needs and the host site's needs can be successfully married.

Part-time interns, on the other hand, do not generally have company resources personally assigned to them but rather are more likely to share whatever resources are available. Full-time or part-time, dedicated resources or shared resources, the important consideration is the communal and professional experiences shared by interns, their supervisors, and host sites. Such communal experiences promote social learning and create environments in which Vygotsky's zone of proximal development may more likely be attained.

AFFECTIVE SUPPORT

While logistical support is important to the intern's success, the affective support provided can be as important, if not more so. Because the application of certain aspects of social learning theory to internships in such a way that create opportunities for communality and shared learning between interns and their supervisors, providing affective support for interns becomes a key element in supervisory responsibilities. In most professional organizations, intern supervisors are the primary sponsors for interns. They give of themselves, their knowledge, and experience, and use their influence to help interns grow during the internship, whether it be by directly instructing the interns or indirectly providing them with the resources they need or serving as a model of professional comportment. Supervisors of successful internships, therefore, must allocate sufficient time to the interns' supervision. This is so critical to internships' success that if supervisors do not feel they will be able to commit sufficient time to provide their interns with necessary affective support, it would be wise for them not to sponsor an internship.

However, in some cases we have seen a middle ground effectively reached. Useful strategies to avoid a potential lack of affective support include having the designated supervisor delegate the day-to-day oversight of interns to other employees whom they also supervise. In some ways, this can even enhance social learning by expanding the group of professionals who are directly accessible to and responsible for interns, while concurrently extending the zone of proximal development to include interns and professionals in the same supportive community. This scenario certainly stands greater chances of success if these second-tier employees, to whom supervisory responsibility for an intern is delegated, understand the professional benefits of the situation rather than merely believing unasked-for additional work is being foisted on them.

Part of the affective support provided in internships is determined when the level of professional experience the site can provide is matched with the needs, abilities, and interests of the intern. Because of the level of their previous training and education, some interns would be more comfortable in roles that required them to be observers of the professional work at their internships. And in other situations, this observer role may be all that is allowed by labor agreements that are in place at the company or in the industry. Still other interns, who possess sufficient skills, will want to help with the professional work of their host site. This is, in fact, the goal we have for all our internships. But here, too, careful screening of potential interns is required to match the site's needs and possibilities with the interns' desires. Some sites, while recognizing interns' ambitions for independent projects, cannot allow them to take on client projects, but may be in a position to allow them to either observe or develop client projects that are presented to the supervisor but not to the client; or the intern may be allowed to develop projects that have an internal client at the host site. Each of these has been used successfully at internships we have overseen in the past.

Assisting an intern in understanding and adapting to the prevailing corporate culture of the host site is also an aspect of providing affective support, as well as drawing upon the benefits of social approaches to learning. New interns will be strangers to the organization, bringing with them all the common disorientation that such new experiences entail. They will need to be oriented to how things work within the organization, where things are, what the professional expectations are, as well as any codes of conduct, dress codes, or security procedures they need to follow.

Orienting interns to job descriptions is an important aspect of creating a comfortable work environment and establishing professional-level expectations from the start. Such an orientation can help prevent potential miscommunication later, as well as help ensure the success of ongoing internship supervision.

SUPERVISION

Carefully supervising interns is one of the most important activities the host engages in. It is a mentoring relationship between would-be and established professionals that is the foundation for successful internships.

The first aspect of internship supervision should actually happen long before interns are accepted. The host site should create thorough job descriptions for each internship they offer, similar to the job descriptions they would use in hiring professionals, so that potential interns and directors can evaluate possibilities. These descriptions also provide useful starting points in the interviewing process that precedes many internships. Students who are less than sure about what they want from an internship can then at least be able to respond to the job description in determining if their skills and an internship match. As a result, internship descriptions can form the first step in students' research into internships and host sites—both of which provide vital information to prepare for and support the job interview. These activities lead to a two-step process that potential interns and their supervisors may use in determining the fit in an internship: evaluating the site and evaluating the prospective intern.

Once interns are engaged by the host site, they will need to become well-versed in the written and unwritten rules of the site. If there are orientation programs for new employees, wise internship supervision would suggest sending the intern to those programs as well. Many of the sites with which we have experience spend considerable time up front to train interns, similar to how they would train entry-level employees. Not only is this ideal, it can also be the foundation for an ongoing process of continual learning that progresses throughout the internship.

Supervision early in the internship should include an orientation to the department that the intern has joined in order to generate an understanding of the functioning of the department and the intern's role in it. Departments and supervisors accomplish this in several ways. Sometimes the intern is asked to spend a certain amount of time with department members and gradually participate in low-level tasks. Contrary to appearances, this is not an unprofessional expectation of an intern or for internships, despite our strong commitment to the ideal that internships be based on professional experiences. Rather, it is a vital aspect of supervising the intern's orientation to the corporate environment of the host site. For example, an assignment to make 10 copies of a report will require the intern to find and operate the copier and maybe even to figure out how to get more paper if the copier runs out, how to deal with copier malfunctions, and so forth. This gradual participation in the day-to-day enterprise of the host site introduces the processes and people that interns will need to interact with as they are assigned more responsible tasks. Moreover, it provides a low-risk opportunity for interns to prove themselves and thereby earn more professional tasks.

As long as menial work is balanced with professional learning opportunities, the intern will be making important progress toward becoming a fully functional professional in his or her field.

As interns gradually prove their capabilities, more and more professional work should be assigned to them. Not having enough to do is a complaint that indicates a site is not living up to its potential. However, even in the best-run corporate environments, there are times when professionals are not as busy as at other times. It is natural that such circumstances will confront interns as well. In such situations, supervisors should encourage interns to work on their own projects, using the time and facilities of the site. This ensures that the professional training and learning aspects associated with internships continue, even through the slow times.

Because interns will not necessarily assume that doing their own work during less busy times is acceptable, supervisors should explain that it is, encourage it, and be willing to respond to it as part of the internship. Independent thinking and independent work are important aspects of professional growth. The type of independent work we frequently encourage interns to engage in while they are on internship includes their résumé, portfolio, and associated job search activities. One site, a postproduction house in the film industry with which we have had a long and productive relationship, consistently structures their internships so that 60% of the intern's time is spent on the corporate activities of the organization, while the remaining 40% can be devoted to allowing the intern access to state-of-the-art online editing equipment for work on personal film projects.

In addition, not all interns can be expected to be hired at their sites, so having supervisors coach them through the process of looking for their first paid professional position is a particularly valuable learning experience to provide. And supervisors are in a good position to provide such mentoring to interns. They have possibly hired people before and have been exposed to a number of résumés; they have put together their own résumés and have been through the hiring process at least once. Their experience provides an excellent foundation for responding to the interns' job search preparations. They also may have much more of an "ear to the ground" by way of networking in their disciplines so as to be able to advise interns of possible career opportunities in their own or other companies. In some cases, the professional experience of the supervisor may provide different perspectives than the experiences and teaching of faculty. We have seen this particularly in aspects of résumé, portfolio, and application letter design. All of this is valuable input for interns; as they make the transition to practicing professionals, they come to realize that there are frequently no "right" answers to certain problems. They, like all professionals, must learn to weigh the advantages and disadvantages of several courses of action—from deciding on the design of a résumé to deciding on the best course for developing a project—before making a decision.

In order to help interns develop a professional network of their own beyond their classmates, supervisors can direct interns to professional development opportunities, professional organizations, trade publications, and professional conferences that may help them develop professionally beyond their college experiences and to gain entrance into their own professional networks. We have seen the generosity of supervisors extended beyond normal expectations, from professional portfolio reviews to conference trips.

Another important aspect of internship supervision includes any instruction, demonstration, counseling, and critiquing that site supervisors need to do or arrange for others to do. Interns, just as is the case of entry-level employees, will encounter issues that they will need help with. Each organization has its own particular approach to performance, tools, and techniques, and these need careful explanation to interns. Supervisors need to encourage interns to ask questions, and if the internship environment is large or particularly busy, regular times should be set for doing this. Interns who do a lot of work independent of their supervisors will feel more reassured if there are times set aside for their needs. That way they can save up their questions and not feel like they are constantly interrupting the supervisor. If on the other hand, interns work closely with their supervisors in the more classic apprentice relationship, special times for questions are not necessary; those opportunities exist continually. This sort of apprenticing/practice combination is the core of what builds the confidence in an intern, which is critical to professional self-image. In such arrangements, if supervisors do not feel that their interns are making sufficient progress, a consultation may uncover the reasons for a delay in their expected development.

In addition to learning the tools and techniques involved in their chosen professions, interns will learn about the appropriate behavior in dealing with business relationships. Often supervisors include interns in meetings. To prepare them for these experiences, supervisors should inform them about expected behavior at those meetings and whether it is appropriate for them to be included to observe or to participate. Even eager, outspoken interns must realize that there are some situations wherein they will need to save their thoughts and observations for a later time, but they may need to be told which situations those are.

One final aspect of internship supervision can be important to interns. If an internship has been successful, it is our hope and recommendation that supervisors consider writing letters of reference for the interns they host. Most interns have a pretty good sense of what their chances are of getting a positive letter of recommendation from their site supervisor and will ask only if they think it will be a positive recommendation. Site supervisors should expect to be asked for such a letter toward the end of the internship and should therefore think about whether they could recommend the intern and try to collect specific data that could be used as the basis of such a letter. This letter can be seen as one form of summative evaluation of the internship experience; as such, it could be based on reexamining the objectives of the particular internship and determining how well they were met.

SUCCESSFULLY ADMINISTERING INTERNSHIPS

While there are undoubtedly any number of methods by which a host site might administer an internship to promote the types of social learning we advocate, one method that has worked particularly well in our experience is the Internship Agreement (see Appendix 1a and 1b for samples of this agreement). The purpose of this agreement, which is loosely contractual between the site and the intern, is to specify the expectations of the internship, the learning objectives, and the methods by which those objectives are to be met. The agreement is divided into three sections:

- Description of general responsibilities and/or activities
- Statement of learning objectives (what the intern wants to learn)
- Identification of tasks and strategies (how the intern will attain the objectives)

We encourage both interns and supervisors to be as thorough as possible when completing this agreement and to focus on the internship as a learning experience, and we highly recommend that the agreement be discussed and completed during a meeting at which both supervisor and intern are present. Two examples will bear out how valuable the agreement can be when it is approached from this perspective. In each case, one can see that there is a transition of professional work expectations that has been carefully conceived in order to mentor interns from the student levels of knowledge and expertise with which they enter internships to the professional standards necessary for success within their disciplines. The first example is from a high-end motion graphics firm.

Descriptive Title of Internship: Production Intern

Description of general responsibilities and/or activities
Assist producers, designers, editorial and composite artists with post production. Master the machine room for internal client tape duplication. Help maintain client review sites by posting Quicktimes and audio for the client. Assist with receptionist duties when needed.

Statement of learning objectives (what the intern wants to learn)
The intern is eager to learn the ins and outs of a project from conception to completion. He wants to gain an understanding of 3D animation, while gaining more experience with Final Cut Pro and developing skills with Flame.

Identification of tasks and strategies (how the intern will obtain the objectives)
The intern will have the opportunity to sit in on project meetings internally and involving clients. These will include creative sessions, voice-overs, and mixes, as well as other opportunities as they arise. During down time, the intern can observe staff members and gain a better understanding of what is involved in project conception and development. The intern will also shadow designers and have the opportunity to ask questions regarding procedures, leading to the point where he is capable of starting and completing design-related tasks on his own.

By examining these three sections from an Internship Agreement, one can see that they almost ideally meet the standards we have been advocating for promoting social learning and for mentoring an intern to the point of a fully functional professional. In other words, this agreement captures the essence of the benefits of learning by experience. For example, the general description of the internship clearly identifies the level of professional work expected of the intern. Interns at this site are relied upon to be contributors to the design teams. All interns we have sent there do in fact master the processes of creating duplication materials for clients. During periods that they are less busy, they participate in welcoming the public, clients, and potential clients to the facility. And most importantly, once they have proven their mettle in these more introductory tasks, interns participate in the actual production of this company's product. The best of our interns have actually progressed to the point of designer by the completion of the internship, and if the economy supported it, have been hired by the company. As a result, this internship is constructed to inculcate within the intern a sense and appreciation of what it means to be a practicing professional within this field. It is the modern-day equivalent of what would have been thought of 700 years ago as being introduced to the mysteries of the craft.

The intern's desired learning objectives are a little more focused on the hands-on specifics of the profession, but even here a desire to learn what it means to be a professional within his chosen discipline is evident. He points out in his first sentence that he wishes to learn what it means to bring a design project from conception to delivery. Assumed within this desire is the expectation of learning how design teams operate to bring about these tasks successfully.

The final section clearly specifies how the learning objectives will be attained. Here, too, the emphasis is on careful observation and mentored participation in the professional activities of this discipline. And one can tell from the description that the process by which this learning will take place is carefully embedded in the activities planned for the internship.

A second example, this one from a film company that produces award-winning advertisements for television, demonstrates similar approaches to administering a successful internship.

> **Descriptive title of internship: Production Assistant**
>
> **Description of general responsibilities and/or activities**
> Interns are given the opportunity to serve as production assistants on shoots, as well as assisting in all aspects of pre-production work. General responsibilities include assisting production staff members, performing research, updating and creating director's reels using Avid, Photoshop, and DVD Studio Pro, as well as helping with office maintenance and organization.
>
> **Statement of learning objectives (what the intern wants to learn)**
> The intern is looking to gain adequate production experience to prepare himself to join the working film community. With the internship, he hopes to gain on-set experience as well as learn how a commercial production comes to fruition from bidding to production to post-production.
>
> **Identification of tasks and strategies (how the intern will attain the objectives)**
> The intern will attain these objectives by working firsthand with the production staff and by integrating himself into the daily work flow of a commercial advertising production house.

Here, too, there are many important aspects of how the site has chosen to administer its internship. Once again, the expectations for the intern range from the introductory tasks of familiarizing himself with the company and its daily work procedures, including "office maintenance"—a euphemism for cleaning up. Because, as has been pointed out earlier in this book, we seek internships that place a premium on professional work, one of our interns asked his supervisor about cleaning up. The supervisor responded that "since the president of our company empties the dishwasher, it is probably not beneath the dignity of an intern to do it too." And as one can surely tell, the responsibilities described in this agreement do, in fact, place a premium on professional work. But more to the point, participating in even the mundane daily activities of running a small, entrepreneurial, and highly successful commercial advertising company is an aspect of social learning that is important to success in any such company within this discipline. As a result, in addition to office maintenance, interns are expected to be contributing members of the production team, filling the important role of production assistant. This requires them to know the ins and outs of film production (skills they have learned during their academic preparation for this internship), to be self-sufficient in the often harried atmosphere of on-set production, and to be accurate in the completion of their duties. Interns at this site regularly perform preproduction site research by helping to determine and schedule locations for film shoots.

These activities dovetail nicely with what the intern has expressed as his learning objectives. He directly expresses a desire to learn what is required to become part of a community, in his case the professional film community, thereby identifying specifically the types of social learning we have pointed out as core principles of successful internship programs. The intern is, in other words, seeking admittance into a practicing community of professionals.

Finally, the tasks and strategies that have been identified for the intern to participate in so that he attains his goals succinctly describe the learning-by-doing nature of becoming a member of this community. The intern is expected to become part of "the daily work flow."

To the credit of both of these sites, they are excellent examples of the theory of internships worked out in practice. They represent the ideals of creating a milieu in which social learning can take place. And in each case, they have provided extraordinary experiences for the interns that we have sent there over a period of 15 years. Almost all of them are now practicing professionals in their fields. Some were hired by the companies at which they interned, and others have gone on to successful film and animation careers in Hollywood and elsewhere.

CONCLUSION

As we have seen in this chapter, successful internship experiences, both for the intern and for the host site, depend heavily on recognizing that there are certain administrative responsibilities sites would do well to meet. Establishing a secure foundation for the internship goes a long way toward avoiding unnecessary confusion and mistakes that any new interns might be prone to make. Moreover, meeting those responsibilities fosters the creation of an environment in which learning and professional growth are foremost, an environment in which the zone of proximal development can rightfully be expected to diminish as interns progress toward becoming fully functional professionals in their discipline. The two examples presented here are but a small portion of the many that exemplify ways to attain these goals. In each case, over periods of many years, these internship sites have been successful in mentoring interns through the transitional process from student to practicing professional. In doing so, they have provided their interns with extraordinary examples of discipline-based excellence in collegial communities of practice *(praxis)*. Upon this, successful careers are built.

CHAPTER 6

Internship Preparation

Mentoring is great when the mentor is great.

Susan Templeton
North Central Massachusetts Chamber of Commerce

In previous chapters, we examined the academic and internship host site responsibilities regarding internships. In many ways, those issues touched upon the subject of internship preparation, particularly the material that concerned academic responsibilities. But in each of those previous chapters, the viewpoint was from a perspective other than that of students. In the first case, an underlying issue of academic responsibilities has to do with accountability of educational institutions. For some years now, institutions of higher learning have grappled with an increased focus on outcomes assessment. We believe that properly designed and managed internships, especially those that serve as the capstone graduation requirement in a curriculum, provide excellent support for defending a program's outcomes by clearly demonstrating a student's grasp of academic material combined with a requisite knowledge and utility to put what they have learned into practice within a discipline of the student's choosing. In the second case, an underlying issue with regard to hosting internships is a concern for having the experience be productive not only for students but for the host sites as well. Developing strategies to assure this will also help ensure that relationships between academic institutions and their host internships remain healthy for a long time.

In this chapter we focus on the responsibilities of students as they consider and prepare for internships. These responsibilities include:

- Approaching the work in every preprofessional course as having the potential to create valuable portfolio materials
- Examining work in theoretical and non-preprofessional courses for its application to one's career preparation
- Researching potential internship sites that appeal to students and fit into their professional or postgraduate plans
- Foreseeing the financial demands that unpaid, full-time internships place upon students
- Participating fully in all internship preparation and qualification programs
- Developing the maturity required to successfully engage in internships

PREPROFESSIONAL COURSEWORK AS PORTFOLIO MATERIALS

Whether students major in business, prelaw, premedicine, engineering, the sciences, the social sciences, communications, or other branches of preprofessional college majors, the work they create in their major courses is an excellent resource for portfolio materials. Students whose course of study includes or leads to a culminating internship experience need to be made aware of the necessity for treating every preprofessional course and the assignments therein as such a resource. Our experience shows that at times this is a difficult concept for entering freshmen to grasp, but those who do avert needless work and worry later in their college careers when they are attempting to find suitable entries for their portfolios. Reports, lab documents, short films, prototype designs, course papers—all of these can demonstrate the accomplishments of students during their academic courses of study and map their growth as individuals. When organized into a well-thought-out portfolio, they also support the students' readiness to engage in an internship.

Some of the best of these portfolios include professional work accomplished by students while still students. Some have worked on independent films, for which they received a credit; some have experience as professional wedding photographers; some have designed CD covers and related artwork for local rock bands; some have designed Web sites, both personal and professional; some have been freelance editors; others have worked in a variety of businesses and industries. Many, if not most of these experiences have produced artifacts that are suitable as portfolio material. Not that long ago, a photography student in our department, while preparing for his portfolio defense, was discussing the photographs he should include in his portfolio. All of the shots had been taken to meet requirements in various photography courses he took as an undergraduate. He happened to mention that, as a member of the New Hampshire National Guard, he was a veteran of the war in Iraq, as well as having been stationed in New Orleans as part of the rescue and recovery mission following hurricane Katrina. He had some photographs from both experiences and wondered if they should be considered for his portfolio. In short, those photographs were searing examples of photojournalism, far better than anything he had produced in his academic courses. And of course, we encouraged him to redesign his portfolio to reflect a serious talent and interest in photojournalism. The portfolio led to an internship in a regional newspaper and eventually to a career as a photojournalist.

In addition to considering the appropriateness of artifacts from professional responsibilities as potential portfolio material, many academic departments, colleges, and universities host a variety of annual juried exhibitions of student work. In our department at Fitchburg State College, the annual Visions exhibition is considered by most students and faculty as the culmination of the best work students have created during the year. Competition for having work selected is intense, and the best work chosen almost always becomes a student's key portfolio piece.

The primary consideration in having students think long-term about materials that might eventually be in their professional portfolios is to inculcate in them early in their college careers a sensitivity for what might be portfolio-calibre work and to seriously consider every assignment, part-time professional responsibility, volunteer position, and so on as providing an opportunity to produce such work. That way, students will have a wealth of materials from which to choose once it is time to build the portfolio.

NON-PREPROFESSIONAL COURSEWORK AS PORTFOLIO MATERIALS

But what about students who major in liberal arts fields? Even here, the movement toward using portfolios as an assessment tool has been successful, but students might need advice in demonstrating their capabilities using materials from such courses. For example, course research papers, poems, fiction, creative nonfiction, expository writing—all can be used effectively to support students' abilities to think creatively, solve complex problems, evaluate and use data, reason, and write clearly. There are very few fields in which such abilities are not a core component of professional success.

For both preprofessional and non-preprofessional coursework, the design and layout of a portfolio helps make it a clear and persuasive statement about the student who presents it. While there are perhaps countless designs available, the one we have developed over the years is actually derived from technical communication practices, especially those that were first made popular nearly 20 years ago with the advent of modular design in manuals [1]. Students' hard-copy portfolios are designed so that each entry functions as an open two-page spread in a longer document. The left-hand page provides the title and type of entry, along with a brief summary that explains why it was chosen, the context of the project from which it was selected, and the skills, knowledge, and abilities it demonstrates. The right-hand page is a sample page from the entry itself. If the entry is a multiple-page document, we advise students to select a page that shows a range of abilities and then place the entire document at the end of the portfolio for easy access, should the person to whom they are showing their work wish to see more of a particular entry. For a sample of this strategy used in hard-copy portfolios, see Appendix 9. More and more students, however, are adopting new presentation technologies to demonstrate their portfolios. These include laptop-based portfolios and, increasingly, CDs and DVDs. Laptop presentations work very well for certain types of portfolio materials, including Web designs, multimedia documents, film, graphic designs, artwork, and so forth. They work reasonably well for text-based portfolio materials, although reading from a laptop is still less than an ideal exercise, even with the latest display technology. CDs and DVDs have an additional advantages over laptop presentations: they are inexpensive enough that prospective interns or employees can leave samples of their portfolios with the persons who have interviewed them.

Students in our program defend these portfolios before a faculty committee. In these 30-minute presentations, the prospective interns display and explain the contents of their portfolios, reasons why the artifacts presented represent their best professional work and abilities, and how these artifacts relate to their internship and eventual career goals. As mentioned earlier, one of the preparatory seminars is devoted entirely to preparing prospective interns for their portfolio defense. Models are demonstrated, and faculty representing each discipline explain what is to be expected in a professional portfolio in that discipline.

Another of the preparatory seminars is devoted to designing and developing résumés. Their presentation is also part of the portfolio-defense session. While there is an infinitude of potential résumé designs, for the purposes of securing internship placement, we have focused on a relatively traditional format that includes an objective as the first entry. We feel that section is particularly important because in it students are expected to identify that they are applying for an internship (as opposed to a paying professional position), the field in which the internship should reside, how it takes advantage of and builds upon their previously attained skills and knowledge, and how it will prepare them for successful future employment in their chosen profession. The rest of the résumé is relatively standard; it includes a section on education, related professional experience, honors, and interests. While résumés are vitally important to the internship application process, we hope that with adequate preparation, students will arrive at the portfolio defense with a résumé that is as close to perfect as possible; accordingly we provide models for them to follow (see Appendix 7). Careful proofreading on the part of students and a willingness of department faculty to review drafts of résumés, helps to ensure that the time we spend correcting the résumé is minimal, allowing more time for a thorough presentation and defense of the portfolio.

RESEARCHING POTENTIAL INTERNSHIP SITES

Any time prior to internship qualification and placement, students should be encouraged to think about and even research potential internship sites that they might want to consider later in their academic careers. This research can take many forms. If an internship program has been long established at a college or university or even within an academic department, students can examine past records of previous internships and learn about companies from the perspective of former interns. That is a resource we readily provide to our students. Students also regularly use the World Wide Web for research purposes, but the information that is available to them is limited by the quality of the Web site. At best, students are able to develop a feel for a company or organization by examining how they present themselves on the Web. At worst, we have had numerous experiences, particularly in the graphic design and Web design fields, in which students have located what seems to be a reasonable prospect for an internship only to learn that the site is in reality a one-person company run out of a bedroom or garage.

Other possible sources for information about companies and organizations include the reference sections in college libraries. Despite the reliance of an entire generation upon Web-based information resources, libraries remain an excellent resource for a wide range of company-based materials, as do college and university career-placement departments. In addition, there are numerous publications on hand at any well-stocked bookstore that provide nearly endless information on job hunting or internship hunting in virtually any discipline. Serious students should be encouraged to explore all of these resources to learn more about and prepare for internships.

FORESEEING THE FINANCIAL DEMANDS OF INTERNSHIPS

If colleges adopt a nonpaying internship program or programs that permit students to be placed in internships that are located at considerable distances from the college, then the internship will inevitably place a financial burden on some students. The earlier they understand that burden, the better they are able to plan for it. Since we have employed a program that is both unpaid and allows our best students to engage in internships at locations around the country and increasingly internationally, we begin communicating the financial cost to students prior to their matriculation as freshmen. We assume that one of the components of our program that attracted them to our college was the required internship, and part of their freshmen orientation includes an overview of what the program entails. It is always disappointing to see a student have to decline an opportunity to intern at the BBC, a major Hollywood film studio, or any other excellent though expensive internship because they have not planned for the cost.

Useful information to provide to students includes the cost of living at a variety of potential sites. We regularly send students to Los Angeles, New York, Atlanta, and Washington DC. As a result, we provide information packets that include such specifics as the cost of apartment housing in a given location; the cost and availability of mass transit systems; the cost and average commuting times for internship locations, such as Los Angeles, that require students to have their own transportation; the cost of food and incidentals, and so forth. This information allows students to both plan long-range for the internships they hope to obtain and to factor cost into their eventual internship decisions. Wise planning on the part of students, along with accurate advice from faculty and program administrators, leads to internship decisions that meet students' professional needs as well as their financial realities.

PARTICIPATING FULLY IN INTERNSHIP QUALIFICATION PROGRAMS

In a competitive internship environment, everything students do factors into the decision regarding placement. Consequently, it is in the best interest of students to approach qualification programs seriously. Their professional future literally depends upon it. The students who do so learn that by the time they complete the qualification process and are defending their professional portfolios before a faculty committee, the experience is not so much one of defense and correction as it is a professional conversation among colleagues. That is always our goal, and a large percentage of students attain it. But at times, we have found the portfolio defense to bog down in corrections of résumés, portfolio designs, and questions about why certain portfolio decisions were made. Compared with what a portfolio defense can be, relegating it to those types of experiences wastes the time of all involved—especially because each of those issues could have been resolved prior to the defense—and negatively affects the students' chances for obtaining the internship.

DEVELOPING THE MATURITY TO BE A SUCCESSFUL INTERN

Internship, viewed in the manner that has been presented here, assumes that students enter as mature, competent, preprofessionals who will use the internship to develop the experience necessary to compete successfully in the job market of their disciplines. Anything less than that fails to reap the full benefits of what internships have to offer. Developing that maturity is an evolutionary process that must include curriculum prior to internship. In all of our professional courses, students are encouraged to treat their work as professional performance. Because placement in our sites is competitive, the best students realize that securing a top internship is their responsibility. The sites with which we work also realize this, and some (especially those that have employees who graduated from our program) actively recruit our top candidates, vetting them in the process.

Becoming a member of a community of practice under the tutelage of established professionals is, as we have pointed out previously, a type of learning to which more and more disciplines have productively returned. Students, faculty, and professionals sharing in the expectations for internships can be (and should be) among the best ways for young persons to become lifelong learners and enter successfully into learning organizations.

REFERENCE

1. Weiss, E. *How to Write a Usable Users Manual.* Phoenix, AZ: Oryx Press, 1986.

CHAPTER 7

Internship Performance Evaluation

When I evaluate the performance of interns, I always keep in mind to take a deep breath and remind myself that I'm dealing with a college student and not a compensated employee. Interns are just crossing through an enormous lifestyle change, and some adjustment to the real world of television is to be expected. Matching a client's rhythm can be tricky in a creative environment, and as a result, I focus on the intern's social skills as well as professional training. This balance keeps me sharp, as well as the intern, and it allows me to determine right away how much more I can expect of the intern and what level of advanced tasks I can push toward by the end of the internship.

Harris Upham
PowPix Productions

Since internships combine aspects of academic coursework and professional experience—a confluence of *episteme*, *techne*, *praxis*, and *phronesis*—it stands to reason that evaluating the intern's performance should also combine aspects of matching course assignments to pedagogical objectives and matching on-the-job performance with appropriate entry-level professional objectives. In this chapter, we consider methods for evaluating both academic and professional performance. In doing so, we are assuming the model of an academic credit-granting internship that has been developed throughout this book.

ACADEMIC CONTENT AND EVALUATION

Whether colleges decide to grant three or six credits for part-time internships or grant twelve credits for full-time internships, if credit is to be granted, academic content should be considered necessary. But what sort? Is there an epistemic content to internships? If so, what is it and how can students' mastery of it be evaluated? For example, the first chapter of this book could be assigned, but does imparting this knowledge have value in an internship where the focus is rightly, it seems to us, on aspects of *techne, praxis*, and *phronesis*? Different colleges, universities, and academic departments will come to different conclusions regarding these issues, but curricular discussions of them should be included in developing any internship program.

Our experience with full-time credit-granting internships that function as the capstone graduation requirement has led us to believe that appropriate academic content should require student interns to tap into the full range of their previous academic experiences in order to reflect on how such experiences inform and explain what they have observed and accomplished while on internship. In an era when more and more colleges struggle with ways to create valid outcomes-assessment strategies, our internship has always functioned as such—even before there was such a term and such an interest. Incorporating internships of this sort into a variety of curricula at virtually any college or university is a viable method for assessing the outcomes of the college's and individual department's programs, particularly when such assessments are combined with the statistics of placement of graduates into professional positions or graduate schools. All that is needed is to fashion the academic content of internships so that it reflects upon the prior academic content of the instructional department, college, or university.

For example, in the Department of Communications Media at Fitchburg State College, students combine a significant theoretical foundation, which extends over their four years, with their professional coursework. As a result, most students have had coursework in cognate areas such as organizational communication, interpersonal communication, communication law and ethics, gendered communication, human communication, mass communication, systems theories, message design, and so forth. We expect them to recognize and utilize the connections between these theoretical concerns and their professions. The internship's academic content is where these expectations bear fruit.

Student interns, therefore, have a variety of course assignments that span the semester of internship. They revise their résumés from the academic version used for internship placement to a version appropriate for applying to their first professional position (*praxis* and *phronesis*). In accomplishing this, they are mentored by both their college internship supervisor and their professional supervisor at the internship site (*techne* and *praxis*). Once that has been accomplished, they are required to identify a potential job (or graduate school, if that is more appropriate) to which they might be interested in applying. Again, using the coaching of both of their supervisors, they craft an application letter (or in the case of graduate school applications, a full application packet) that will accompany their revised résumés (*praxis* and *phronesis*). We do not require them to actually apply for either the position or graduate school, but should they wish to, they will be fully qualified to.

Our student interns are also required to keep a daily journal of their internship activities (*techne, praxis*, and *phronesis*). We provide them with several forms from which they can choose for the design of their journals (see Appendix 4a), but we also encourage them to design and develop formats that are appropriate to their needs and to the particular type of internship in which they are engaged (*phronesis*). As a result, daily journals can vary from cryptic log entries to full-fledged journals (for an example, see Appendix 4b and 4c). Of late, we have been stressing the full-fledged journal (*phronesis* and *episteme*) because it requires students to be more reflective than the typical cryptic log entries that are forced upon them by a standard form. Our reasoning for this is that such journals, because they include applications of what students have learned in their communication theory classes regarding interpersonal, intercultural, organizational, and gendered communication, better prepare them for the two major final assignments.

The first of these assignments is to write a summary of their daily journals. Although student interns are free to complete this in any form they wish, we recommend a two-column list. The left-hand column summarizes tasks and activities performed while on internship (*techne*), and the right-hand column summarizes the associated learning (*praxis* and *phronesis*) developed from those activities (see Appendix 5).

The second major assignment is essentially a culmination of the students' internship experience. It is a research paper that brings to bear their theoretical coursework onto their professional internship experiences (*episteme*, *praxis*, and *phronesis*). The assignment is to research the history, structure, and culture of their internship site and to reflect upon the health and stability of the organization while making predictions regarding its future. This becomes a significant academic experience for our student interns, one in which they learn as much about themselves as they do about the organization with which they have interned. To assist them in conducting their research, we provide a list of topics and suggestions by which they might approach the assignment (see Appendix 6).

Both of the final assignments become part of our department's formal record of the internship—in terms of outcomes assessment and documenting what occurs at particular sites. If we place future interns at the site, we are then able to provide copies of these assignments to them for review so they can decide if the site holds interest for them.

PROFESSIONAL PERFORMANCE EVALUATION

When we engage an organization for an internship, we expect that supervisors will evaluate the performance of their interns at the conclusion of the internship, and we provide a form for doing so (see Appendix 2b and 2c) which then also becomes part of the official record of the internship. Our experience, as well as independent research by others, suggests that most supervisors and host sites are generally satisfied with the performance of interns. Masson and Pelham reported that "94% of those who had hosted interns in their organization were satisfied or very satisfied with their interns" [1, p. 2]. As a result, it would seem that intern performance does not present a problem for most sites, but one would assume that the cause of this positive finding relates directly to the structure and rigor of evaluation processes at those sites. In this section we describe a process that can be followed to keep the evaluation endeavor positive, supportive, objective, and manageable with as few negative surprises as is possible. The steps in the process include writing objective job descriptions for interns, asking them to contribute their goals for their internships, informing the participants of any additional criteria outside those included in the job description that will be used during evaluations, setting up formative evaluation checkpoints and meetings, and seeking suggestions for improvements of the evaluation process.

Job Descriptions for Interns

In addition to the general description of internships, described in previous chapters, the specific responsibilities and activities that interns will be required to perform should be carefully considered and written out by the host site. Ideally, this would be similar to other job descriptions for employees in that it would follow the format and style utilized in the organization, and it would fulfill a similar purpose in functioning as the basis for performance reviews by providing specific job-related objectives.

There are numerous resources that describe how to develop performance-based objectives for job evaluations, but a brief summary is presented here.

The best way to think about writing performance-based objectives is to ask if what has been written in the job description would be recognized by another person who was observing the performance of the intern. For instance, assume that the job description specifies that interns will "answer the phone." If the interns let the phone ring and ring, they have not achieved that particular objective for their job. On the other hand, if they pick up the phone, they are meeting that objective. But the objective as written does not address the qualitative issues with regard to answering the phone. If the intern picks up the phone and says "yo" into the handset, they are still achieving the objective as stated. To more clearly state the desired objective in performance for the job description, "in a professional manner" could be added, but even this should be defined more specifically. Admittedly, this process of expanding the objective can go on ad infinitum if the person responsible for designing the objective takes nothing as assumed. The performance-based objective for answering the phone could include "stating the intern's name, the department and asking the caller 'how can I help you?'" But if "professional manner" can be recognized by most people to include those details, then they need not be added. Remember, however, that it is best to err on the side of too much information rather than too little.

One form of vague objective often found in job descriptions is the use of the word "assist." For example, a job objective might say "interns will assist in the completion of forms for payment relative to corporate brochures" or "interns will assist on film shoots." If the interns carry the forms from here to there in the first example or move a piece of equipment in the second example, they are technically "assisting," but only at a very rudimentary level. As a result, here too it would be better to add specific details to improve the objective's clarity. In the first instance, perhaps the host organization wants interns to copy and file the forms; maybe they would like interns, by the end of their internship, to be able to initiate the use of the form correctly, complete all information, copy it, send it to all necessary parties, and file it. The more specific the objective, the better; but there will always be a point at which most people would know that behavior if they see it. Deciding on what that point is determines the specificity of the performance-based objective, and often that point is at a lower level for interns than it might be even for entry-level employees.

One objective that might make sense in every statement of performance objectives would be to increase the intern's ability to be an active problem solver. Inkster and Ross suggest that supervisors accomplish this by turning appropriate questions back to the intern, asking them what they think and what they would suggest [2, p. 31]. In other words, when interns ask for advice, it would be of greater educational value to use that as a "teaching moment" by structuring a process in which they can arrive at the correct answers to their questions. Since one of the most important goals of internships is to develop students into fully differentiated professionals in their fields, it would make sense to incorporate such a problem-solving process into the structure of internship supervision and performance evaluation.

By applying these observable and measurable approaches to writing internship job descriptions, the host site and supervisors will be able to determine the intended level of performance more accurately.

Some companies use a management-by-objective (MBO) approach to specifying employee performance criteria and may decide to extend that to internship evaluation. That method also tries to use observable conditions, but it usually sets dates for attaining specific goals under each objective. These programs have as a common central theme the concept that "identified and understood objectives lead to improved performance in organizations. . . . MBO is a system for managing organizations that ties together long-range strategic plans with short-range operating plans" [3, pp. 97-98]. As a result, it would be powerful and educational for interns to understand how their efforts are incorporated into the overall strategic plans and central goals of their internship organization. While minimally, this satisfies the need to have objective characteristics on which to base performance appraisals, beyond that, it inculcates in interns the importance of what they do.

In addition to developing performance-based objectives for an internship job description, it is a good idea to add the goals that the intern has for the internship, thereby emphasizing the learning aspect of the internship. Here again it is important to remember that since interns are not paid employees, they are looking to attain other sorts of goals. These might include producing a report that analyzes the internship experience or creating a portfolio piece that shows the level of skill the intern has been able to achieve. If interns are not working on client-level projects, perhaps they will have access to a project that uses a current client need and be allowed to treat it as a case study, utilizing the resources of the corporation to create their own version of the client project, which could then be evaluated by the intern's supervisor. One of the sites we regularly work with did precisely that for a recent intern. She was a video editor interested in the field of advertising, and the company was working with a major sporting-goods client. The intern was permitted to sit in on all meetings with the client, observing the give-and-take that is typical of creating advertising for television. Afterward, she was instructed to take available footage that the agency was using to create the client's ads and edit it into 30-second formats she felt would be appropriate for the client and for the time slots in which the ads were scheduled to be played. After she completed these tasks, her supervisor carefully critiqued her work. This was a process to which the intern responded particularly well, and by the end of her internship she was permitted not only to observe during meetings but to contribute to them. Some of her suggestions eventually made their way into the final advertisements that were aired on local television stations, thereby significantly adding to her professional portfolio and providing a meaningful foundation for her first steps into her chosen career. Consequently, designing these types of experiences and including them as "intern learning objectives" becomes a useful addition to performance-based internship descriptions.

Following the general job description, the performance-based objectives for the internship, and the intern's learning objectives, a third section that describes the tasks and strategies interns should use to attain objectives should be added. This helps to flesh out the evaluation process and focus it on items that are clearly measurable. Once all of this information is specified, supervisors can turn their attention to formative evaluation concerns, deciding how and when to give ongoing evaluative feedback to the intern. Many supervisors do this on an "as needed" basis. This can be potentially problematic because "as needed" frequently becomes interpreted as "when problems arise." The result is that interns may develop the sense that talking to the supervisor is negative. There are two methods that can counteract this natural tendency. One is to schedule daily or weekly brief meetings with interns to assess performance and progress in job-related assignments. This can be useful in avoiding numerous interruptions for the supervisor as well as assuring interns that they have a certain amount of time to figure out issues on their own, but that there will also be a time to ask for help. The other method is to intentionally find opportunities to provide positive feedback to interns about their performance. Traditionally, this has been an effective human-resource management tool in all types of disciplines. Wysocki and Kepner explored the three types of feedback that are available to a supervisor (negative, none, positive) and concluded that "positive feedback is the only one that will consistently generate the type of worker performance that managers and organizations want" [4]. Moreover, Latting reports that a "4:1 positive to negative feedback ratio is needed to create an optimal work environment" [5]. Correspondingly, the effects of negative feedback have also been studied. One of the major findings in a study by Kay, French, and Meyer was that "the more criticism and defensiveness were observed in the performance discussion, the less performance improvement was achieved 12 to 14 weeks later" [6]. As a result, it appears that to give feedback and to conduct performance appraisals effectively, one has to largely build upon the positive and be careful "to handle problem situations without causing resentment on the part of the subordinate" [7]. One method for accomplishing this is to ensure that supervisors understand why mistakes and problems occur and to use that understanding as the basis for a problem-solving approach to performance appraisals, rather than to criticize.

In order to supervise interns successfully, information must be collected on what the interns are doing and how well they are doing it.

This takes time, energy, and opportunity. If any of these are not available, perhaps other employees could be enlisted to help observe and collect data on interns' performance. As a result, some sites have supervisors assign a person for the intern to go to when the supervisor is busy or when persons other than the supervisor can answer questions.

If there are any evaluation tools, forms, or criteria that will be used to evaluate interns, these should be shared with them at the earliest opportunity. At the time an intern applies for an internship at Fitchburg State College, they learn about the performance-appraisal form that the college requires supervisors to complete. This allows them to know what material on which they will be judged so that they can adapt their performance to meet those performance-based criteria. Our appraisal form is fairly generic and has served our needs for internship evaluation very well. It has a number of questions regarding the intern's qualities to which supervisors may respond, thus determining the level of our interns' accomplishments. It also provides space for comments, which we encourage. This method provides useful data and observations collected over the course of the internship regarding performance.

Maintaining a positive approach with interns, even if the performance appraisal seems to be a negative assessment, is important, as internships are essentially learning experiences, and interns should be expected to learn from their mistakes in order to not repeat them when they are fully functional professionals. Positive approaches to internship evaluation use negative assessments to guide interns toward behaviors and actions that could improve their performance. They also provide them with the opportunity to address problems. Interns are more likely to grow when feedback is presented in a positive and supportive way.

The final aspect of evaluating intern performance is providing suggestions on how to strengthen skills; supervisors are in a unique position to give this advice. Interns choose internships for the opportunity to "reality test" their skills and to grow in their chosen profession. Supervisors play an important role in providing valuable insight and information; it is their feedback that points interns in the right direction toward becoming professionals. In Appendix 1a and 1b, we have provided a sample Internship Agreement, which we have found useful in establishing professional expectations for the internship, as well as the foundations upon which interns are to be evaluated at their host site.

Attitude

Attitude is probably the single most important factor that will come to bear on the performance of the intern. The match between intern and internship should be made on a conscious and honest level so that the attitude of the intern is eager and positive. If interns start to feel less than positive, it is important to figure out what is dampening their enthusiasm. They might have a fantasy version of what their experience and expectations will be, but the reality of actually doing all the hard work that goes into professional endeavors can be a rude awakening.

For many interns, it may be the first time that they have worked 40 hours a week. This alone is enough to shake the fortitude of some, especially since many must have part-time jobs in addition to their internships. In worst case scenarios, we have had interns who successfully balanced a full-time internship with a full-time job, because they were self-supporting throughout college. Figuring out where they will find it within themselves to accommodate all the demands being placed on their time and energy in what turns out to be an 80-hour work week can be a daunting task—one that is best undertaken with the assistance and support of both their academic internship supervisor and their professional supervisor. But in all situations, the interns themselves should take measure of their attitude and be the first to be aware of any changes from positive to negative.

Reflecting on this can be a primary source of learning within the internship experience. If they are given a task that they do not want to do, it can be turned into an opportunity for figuring out what it is about the task that they do not like. And if it is a task that is a large part of the professional field they are considering and preparing for, it will force them to confront whether or not they are in the appropriate field. Self-knowledge of this type will be valuable for a long time to come.

Communication

Beyond a positive personal attitude, the ability to communicate with others is likely to be another important attribute an intern will possess and exercise on a successful internship. Listening to superiors and understanding what tasks are required is critical to performance. Careful listening is a skill that is not often directly taught in institutions of higher education. It is indirectly part of what happens in any college course. Careful listening has several components. Interns need to realize when what is being told to them is important. If they are not sure, they should ask. Asking questions to make sure they understand their instructions is another important component of listening. Many times, the best way to ensure one has heard what has been said is to repeat it back to the speaker. Interns should consider taking notes whenever they are receiving instructions they perceive to be important. Being a careful listener will take interns a long way toward a positive performance. Furthermore, interns should be instructed to never say that they understand something if they are not sure they did. Honesty is important to the communication process.

Once interns have carefully listened and confirmed their understanding of the tasks that they have been asked to perform, the next communication step is to keep their supervisor informed as to how they are doing with those tasks. Interns may want to ask their supervisor who they should ask if they have additional questions. It is very possible that the supervisor would not be the best person to refer some questions to. Interns should ask how the supervisor would like to be kept apprised of the progress of the task. Also asking about related deliverables and their due dates will help the intern perform in a professional manner. Some supervisors may meet with interns on a daily basis. Others will ask that they receive a written report of progress each week or even more infrequently. Understanding the supervisor's expectations for being informed on the progress of assigned tasks will be critical to a positive handling of confidential information during the performance review.

In many organizations, the issue of confidentiality is particularly important. If supervisors do not cover expectations with regard to confidential information, interns should ask to be made aware of any confidential information that they will have access to and how they should handle such information. Students have not usually developed a sense of what might be considered proprietary information within an organization. And different organizations treat the issue in different ways; interns should be instructed in what is appropriate to discuss and what is not. This knowledge becomes an important aspect of their learning experience.

Related to confidentiality with regard to communication is the understanding of how the chain of command is dealt with. Interns need to be aware of how the organization works, particularly with respect to the culture of intra-organizational and hierarchical communication. Generally, they should be encouraged to check with their supervisor before contacting others within the organization. The possibility of erring is real, and the interns need to rely on their supervisor to enlighten them as to "how things are done" within the organization.

Errors and mistakes are going to happen on most internships, therefore interns must learn how to react when they occur. An appropriate and professional strategy is to focus on what happened, how to fix it, and how to prevent it from happening again—rather than focusing on fault or blame. Openness is essential, and interns need to realize that small errors become large ones if covered up. Both co-workers and supervisors can be helpful in exploring and managing mistakes made by the intern. No one is perfect, and sites do not expect interns to be, but they do expect interns to learn from their mistakes and to not repeat them.

Workplaces also serve social functions as well, but how interns fit into the social environment of an internship site varies from organization to organization. Some organizations view interns as separate from their professional employees and do not include them in work-related social activities; others view it differently. At a recent supervisory visit to an advertising company, one of the authors was told that the intern was doing very well professionally. He came to the internship highly qualified, and he performed what was expected of him quickly, efficiently, and well. But he was reluctant to participate in the group lunches that were an important aspect of the culture of this organization. Once he was advised that this, indeed, was part of the internship experience at this site, he participated and benefited from it, because in these informal settings, people generally shared more about their own personal approaches to their profession than they did while in their everyday ongoing tasks. Regardless of an organization's approach to work-based socialization, interns must realize that such activities should not interfere with the work that needs to get done, and that they are expected to keep all social interactions at a professional level.

Inevitably, some interns will come to realize that certain aspects of the internship are creating negative attitudes within themselves regarding specific tasks and perhaps even the profession itself. How they reflect on these experiences can often provide important learning about themselves and their preparedness for a particular profession. Even learning that the profession they thought they were interested in is not right for them is a positive learning experience, especially if it happens on internship rather than in the midst of their first professional position when other obligations (family, finance, etc.) might require they remain in an unrewarding career. After they assess their own feelings and reflect upon the causes of such negative experiences, interns should talk with their professional supervisor and their academic supervisor. This step should not be taken lightly because they need to realize that one possible cause for the experience is simply that it is the nature of the profession. In such cases, there is little that the supervisor can do, other than point out the value of learning this at the beginning of one's professional life.

Attendance

Just as would be the case for an entry-level professional, attendance is a necessary condition of success on any internship. Any schedule alterations or aberrations must be discussed and agreed to well ahead of time. Any time that is missed on the intern's agreed-upon schedule should be made up. On the other hand, there are occasions when the organization may need interns to work beyond their regular schedule, and in our experience, if this does happen, most organizations have some sort of compensatory time system. There are many ways in which such a system might productively work. Some organizations compensate overtime for an intern by reducing the number of expected hours in ensuing weeks; others pay interns at an entry-level rate for overtime work. Both are effective and appropriate. Politically and professionally, when interns are asked to work overtime, it is wise for them to do so, if at all possible. They will be perceived as team players and will develop a clearer sense of the realities of the profession. We have, on rare occasions, had experiences with sites that demanded enormous hours with no compensation beyond the minimum full-time expectations of our internships. In those circumstances, it is appropriate for the academic supervisor to meet with the organization and review expectations to ensure that they are reasonable. Sixty-five-hour weeks for weeks on end without compensation is not an internship, it is servitude.

A final professional aspect of attendance and communication involves illness. If interns are sick or expect to be late, they must realize the importance of calling their supervisor to tell them. Each day they are out, they need to call. Attendance is an important prerequisite to performing well at an internship, and handling it professionally communicates a significant amount about the intern's responsibility and career readiness.

Workload Issues

In some of our internships, we have found that on occasion there is too much work, too little, and even work that is inappropriate for some reason. In each case, interns and academic internship supervisors need strategies to resolve these issues.

When interns believe they have too much work, they should first compare what they are being asked to do with entry-level employees who are performing similar responsibilities. If there is a discrepancy, then they should discuss their perceptions with their supervisor and ask the supervisor to prioritize the assignments so that they will have guidance in what to focus on first. Correspondingly, when they suspect that there will be a problem, interns should be advised to discuss it with their supervisor and not wait until it occurs, particularly if the problem involves a deadline for a task. That gives the supervisor opportunity to reallocate resources if the task is essential.

If interns find they do not have enough work, they should examine their professional environment to see if there is related work they might contribute to. Communicating such an interest to their supervisor proves initiative. Sometimes interns are not kept busy because the small tasks they were given were not performed in such a way as to engender trust, and therefore their performance has not warranted giving them greater responsibilities. Recognizing that this might be the case makes them aware of the level of trust they have engendered among their co-workers and the need to change their behavior in order to create greater trust.

If past performance is indeed the reason for generating too little work and too little responsibility, the intern must be willing to ask for and incorporate suggestions for improvement.

If interns experience ebbs and flows of work, there are three strategies for managing their time productively. One is to seek out projects that need to get done and propose doing them. The second is to ask to use the time to work on their own projects. For example, they could work on their résumés or on their job search or on building portfolio material. The third basic strategy is to work on the improvement of their skills. Some interns turn to reading materials in their field, while others pursue tutorials on software packages that they might be able to utilize in the future. All of these are viable options to make down time productive, but each should be discussed with the site supervisor beforehand.

There are, on rare occasions, times when interns are asked to do work that is not appropriate. For example, this might include personal errands for co-workers or being asked to do anything that is not truthful. Ideally, interns should not be asked to do anything that would not be expected of entry-level professionals. And in the case that interns are asked to perform duties which are either dishonest or violate their personal and professional ethical standards, they should contact their academic internship supervisor immediately.

This recently happened with one of the author's interns, a film major. She had identified an independent documentary site that the department had not used for an internship previously. After standard contacts and discussions regarding internship expectations had occurred, she was placed with the site. Approximately two-thirds of the way through the semester-long internship, the student contacted her academic supervisor to inform him that some of what the small company was doing included falsification of tax records for grant-application purposes. She had been asked to participate. After determining that what the intern reported was most likely true, it was determined that the best course of action would be to remove her from the internship and allow her to complete the final weeks back at the college, focusing on what she had learned and incorporating it into her final analytical paper.

Finally, there may be a time in an unpaid internship when interns feel resentful that the host site is getting free labor while getting paid for the work that interns contribute. This usually occurs when they have reached a point wherein they are spending more time contributing to the progress of work and less time learning how to contribute to the work. In other words, they have attained a level of professional competence that allows their host site to rely on their contributions. Attaining such competency is one of the primary reasons for undertaking internships, and reaching that level is reason for celebration rather than resentment. Advising interns accordingly helps them put all of this in proper perspective.

During the last few weeks of an internship, interns should ask for a letter of recommendation from their supervisor, as well as for introductions to other professionals who might assist and mentor their entry into the profession for which they have prepared.

SUMMARY

This chapter focused on the essential qualities that assure positive internship performance. Matching interns and internship site needs can be greatly enhanced by having a well-developed internship job description. Integrating appropriate professional communication strategies and developing a professional approach to attendance are important aspects of developing into a mature professional ready for entry into a chosen career.

In a larger sense, this book has attempted to explore historical and theoretical foundations for internships by tracing such experiences from ancient times to the present within two frameworks. The first grew out of Aristotle's concern for practical and productive knowledge and how those are constitutive of excellence within communities of practice. The second, social theories of learning, especially those derived from Vygotsky, in many ways grew out of the first. If indeed knowledge industries and the colleges, universities, and academic departments who prepare students for successful careers within them return to an enhanced focus on *techne, praxis*, and *phronesis* (while not diminishing the established importance of *episteme*), and if they design internship programs to inculcate in students both excellence and a sense of professional lives worth living, society will be the benefactor.

REFERENCES

1. G. E. Masson and D. Pelham, A national study of supervisors' perception of student interns, in *The Internship Partnership: A Handbook for Business, Non-Profits, and Government Agencies*, R. P. Inkster and R. G. Ross (eds.). Needham Heights, MA: Simon and Schuster Custom Publishing, 1987.
2. R. P. Inkster and R. G. Ross (eds.), *The Internship Partnership: A Handbook for Business, Non-Profits, and Government Agencies*. Needham Heights, MA: Simon and Schuster Custom Publishing, 1987.
3. R. Henderson, *Performance Appraisal: Theory to Practice*. Reston, VA: Reston Publishing Corporation, Inc., 1980.
4. A. Wysocki and K. Kepner, *Managerial Feedback, Associate Performance, and Eleven Positive Feedback Rules*. Web source: http://www.edis.ifas.ufl.edu/BODY_HR206, June 15, 2004.
5. J. K. Latting, Giving correct feedback: A decisional analysis, *Social Work*, pp. 424-427, September 5, 1992.

6. E. Kay, J. P. French, and H. H. Meyer, *A Study of the Performance Appraisal Interview.* Lynn, MA: Behavioral Research Service at General Electric, 1962. In D. Kirkpatick, *How to Improve Performance through Appraisal and Coaching,* New York: Amacom, 1982.
7. D. Kirkpatrick, *How to Improve Performance through Appraisal and Coaching.* New York: Amacom, 1982.

CHAPTER 8

The Future of Internships

Our goal in this book has been to analyze the history and the theoretical underpinnings of learning-by-doing so that together they establish a foundation for internship programs as colleges and universities enter the twenty-first century. For the most part, this presentation has been a positive one. We are convinced, based on the long and generally successful experience of the internship program we manage, that such approaches to learning make sense for careers in a knowledge economy, that they incorporate the best of students' academic backgrounds into that all-important transition to the world of work, and that as a result they hold much hope for future approaches to higher education. But we would be less than forthright if we did not admit that there are consistent challenges which must be overcome in order for internship programs to be successfully designed and managed. In this final chapter, we shall examine some of those.

INTERNSHIPS AND MANAGED HIGHER EDUCATION

Over the last few years, institutions of higher education have begun to hear about a new administrative tool that purports to incorporate aspects of managed health care into the education profession [1-3]. On the surface, any educator from Socrates to the present would recognize the fallacies involved in these lines of thinking because they shift the focus from educating students to the corporate bottom line of educational institutions. But in an era when the rise of higher education costs, like the similar rise in health-care costs, outstrips the annual rise in the cost of living and other inflationary indices, this is a concern of college and university administrations that is not likely to go away.

One of the tenets of managed higher education involve two statistical analyses, known as course utilization and faculty utilization. Essentially, these analyses are constructed upon the ratio of course enrollment to full enrollment in the course. For example, if a course has a maximum of 25 seats and 20 students are enrolled, then the course utilization ratio for that course is 80% (20/25). Some experts in the field of managed higher education suggest that a course utilization ratio of 90% is required for profitability for that course. Faculty utilization simply adds the course utilization ratios for the faculty person for the entire year.

Such statistical analyses of how courses and faculty are utilized certainly identify the courses and faculty who are popular and unpopular on a campus or in a department; for large courses with high enrollments, this method might make some rudimentary sense for determining the course offerings that are profitable. But for seminars, and we would hold for internships also, there is an important logical flaw in this type of thinking, as well as a consequent flaw in this approach to managing the cost of higher education. For example, if the total number of seats for a section of internship is set by contract at 9 (as it is here at Fitchburg State College), and if the section underenrolls by one student, it is automatically underutilized (8/9 = 88.9%). And with each additional student that it underenrolls, the course utilization and consequent faculty utilization ratios get worse. In fact, the only way that internships can be profitable under this type of course-utilization rubric is for the sections to enroll in factors of nine or for them to overenroll (which might subtly be the administrative point), because anything other than these courses of action will automatically lead to underutilization.

The same problems, utilizing this particular approach to managed education, will obviously occur in any course for which enrollment is limited to totals under ten; these would include seminars at many institutions of higher education. As a result, managed higher education could very well pose a threat to the successful design and administration of bona fide internship programs. And if one accepts that internships are indeed vital to the education of twenty-first-century would-be professionals, then, ipso facto, managed education is a less-than-suitable means by which colleges and universities should manage their enterprise in order to meet the needs of a global-knowledge economy.

THE STUDENT-AS-CUSTOMER FALLACY

For approximately two decades now, management consultants to higher education have been advocating an approach to college administration and instruction that is founded upon viewing students as customers. As a result, college and university presidents have picked up this idea, and it has trickled down through various layers of administrators to department chairpersons. As a philosophy of what occurs and what should occur in higher education, it is precisely backward.

Students are the product of institutions of higher learning; societies are the customer. All students enter into the college or university experience as raw material, which is not equal in terms of its quality. Some students are naturally better endowed for the enterprise of higher education, while others may have been either advantaged or disadvantaged by their prior educational experiences. Four or more years of higher education are then utilized to design and develop an educational outcome for that student in such a way that the product of the educational experience functions well for the next 40 to 50 years, perhaps with minor updates along the way, if one subscribes, as we do, to the belief that lifelong learning is absolutely necessary in the professional environment of the twenty-first century. Can anyone think of any other enterprise that places those high expectations on their products? High technology comes nowhere near achieving it; for example, a five-year-old computer is all but useless. Perhaps the only discipline that is competitive is civil engineering, the products of which—structures—in many cases perform adequately for decades, even centuries (Brooklyn Bridge, Great Wall of China, etc.).

Therefore, what is required is a refocusing correctly on the mission of a college or university education, particularly with respect to how internship programs are designed and managed. It is our hope, and we suspect the hope of most who read this book, that the product of higher education will be individuals who are informed, reflective thinkers; persons who not only are prepared to enter specific professions but who are also prepared intellectually to understand their roles within those professions and the culture and social milieu of those professions to such extent that they are productive contributors and more than adequately qualified to change those professions as economic, intercultural, and educational necessities dictate. By extension, this also presumes the suitability of internships for preparing students to meet the tangible expectations that both they and employers hold for the product of that education; namely, that graduates will be fully prepared to accept and successfully perform the responsibilities of whatever profession they have chosen to enter. If internships continue to meet that objective in the coming century and its quickly changing economy, then a centuries-old tradition will likewise find its place adapted for the future.

INTERNSHIPS WITHOUT HIGHER EDUCATION

But what if internships or apprenticeships are offered outside of or in place of higher education? An early trend we have recently become aware of is that of organizations which provide precisely this experience. Internships are designed to establish a probationary period within a professional discipline during which the intern learns and masters the craft of that discipline. This is not only a model of learning based on the guild apprenticeships of earlier times, it *is* that model. Moreover, it provides most of the benefits that have been outlined in this book, with one vital exception. Internships in place of higher education ignore the value of intellectual pursuit, a value we continue to rigorously support.

Perhaps the twenty-first century will prove to be the end of the college-for-almost-everyone philosophy of education and maturation. Indeed, there are signs of this. Young people today, no doubt due to the high cost, enter into a college education asking many more questions about what that education will prepare them to *do* rather than the learning-for-learning-sake attitude reflected in their parents' generations, who were interested in what higher education would prepare them to *know*. Our concern is that while there are understandable arguments for this view, society as a whole is poorer for it.

Because of this, internships without academic preparation, we fear, will tend to divide society into knowers and doers, intensifying a growing educational and economic stratification. Despite our complete conviction in the value of internships as methods of learning, as ways of entering into communities of practice, and of developing and utilizing collective intelligence, this is a trend we are least sanguine about as we foresee the future of higher education. It relegates the learning available through internships to discipline-specific training rather than to the nourishment of the complete self, mentoring young would-be professionals into reflective, self-aware thinkers who not only can be competent in the expectations of their discipline but who can continuously contemplate improvements in that discipline and improvements in the society that utilizes it.

THE COST OF INTERNSHIP MANAGEMENT

From the perspective of college administrators, internships are certainly not cheap. The student/faculty ratio should be low enough that each student is mentored as an individual by the faculty member who is responsible for that student. At our institution, that ratio, set by a statewide faculty union contract, is 9-1. This means that a class of interns has a maximum of nine students in it. A writing class by comparison, has 18 students, so clearly, one section of internships is twice as expensive as one section of freshman composition.

Administrators, making such a comparison based strictly on the books, might be inclined to ask whether or not internships could be managed and supervised by a member of the college administrative staff, who is generally paid approximately half of an average faculty member. The answer certainly is yes, and many institutions across the country use precisely that approach to manage internship programs, co-op programs, school-to-work programs, and a variety of other learning-by-doing quasi-professional experiences that are part of the academic enterprise. But, and it is an important but, it is our contention—supported by nearly 30 years of experience and the feedback of hundreds of internship sites—that this approach does not provide the richness of experience that is available to students who are mentored and supervised by full-time faculty. The owner and president of one of our longstanding internship sites said it well in a letter to our college president: "My advice to any college or university that was considering developing an internship program would be to follow the Fitchburg State College model" [4]. Such sentiment is not unusual in our experience. We have been told by senior management at corporate institutions across the country and abroad that our interns are, in general, among the best prepared and best supervised of any they employ.

We think part of the reason why this is true has to do with the care and attention that faculty can pay to their interns in a 9-1 student/faculty-ratio environment. At most institutions we have studied that adopt a staff-managed approach to internship design, the staff are responsible for many more interns. Contact with the internship site is often limited to the completion of forms and perhaps a telephone call. Contact with interns is limited to a general meeting or two to outline expectations. Interns often find their own internship, sometimes out of a catalog that the college office of internships has available. There are no on-site internship supervisory visits and, as a result, very little interaction between the college and the provider of the professional experience. In this environment, which is common to many institutions of higher education, outcomes are hard to predict. Some students have excellent experiences, while others have the experiences we have assiduously avoided for three decades—photocopying and coffee making.

So, yes, internships—particularly those founded upon the principles we espouse—are not cheap: excellence rarely is.

REFERENCES

1. P. Broderick, From managed care to managed education: How should we seize the day? *Family Medicine, 39*, pp. 324-325, May 1998.
2. C. Thomas, *What's Ahead for Distance Education Students?* www.petersons.com, 2006.
3. H. Mosely, *The Population and Health Materials Working Group: Distance Education.* www.hipnet.org/conf2/distance.htm.
4. A.-M. Aigner, Letter to the President of Fitchburg State College, 2003.

Appendixes

APPENDIX 1a.
Internship Agreement Form

The Internship Agreement form is used to establish both academic (learning) expectations and professional duties for student interns. We encourage internship supervisors and interns to discuss and complete the form together, so that agreements can be reached regarding specific objectives and how they may be attained. Ideally, the agreement provides a general description of the internship, along with the formal title of the position. These two pieces of information help to establish the professional aspects of what the internship entails, and it is hoped that such a description will clearly capture the nature of the transition from student to practicing professional. Beginning with introductory responsibilities, the description should progress to the establishment of what entry-level professionals in the field are assumed to do.

The agreement should also be used by the intern to specify precisely what he or she wishes to learn from the experience. These learning objectives should take into account not only the professional skills that one would expect to hone but also the cultural aspects of participating as an intern in one's chosen profession. This section should include observable and measurable objectives.

The final section of the form should identify the specific strategies and tasks that the intern will be expected to perform in order to attain the learning objectives. The clearer these tasks can be described the easier it is to determine, upon completion of the internship, whether or not they have been met.

Appendix G
Internship Agreement

This agreement is to be completed within the first two weeks of the internship.

Student's Name: ______________________ I.D.#: ______________

Current Address: ______________________ Current Phone#: ______________

Organization's Name: ______________________________________

Address: ______________________________________

On-Site Supervisor: ______________________ Title: ______________

Phone#: ______________________ Extension: ______________

Descriptive title of internship: ______________________________________

Description of general responsibilities and/or activities:

Statement of learning objectives (what the intern wants to learn):

Identification of tasks and strategies (how the intern will attain the objectives):

Time span on internship (dates): From: ______________ To: ______________

Minimum daily work hours of internship:

Mon. ______ Tues. ______ Wed. ______ Thur. ______ Fri. ______ Sat. ______ Sun. ______

The undersigned have read and agree to all the conditions set forth. Furthermore, the on-site supervisor agrees to provide the intern with an orientation concerning relevant organizational policies, procedures and functions, to manage the intern's work assignments, to meet with the intern regularly, and to be available for counsel and advice during the internship. He/she also agrees to participate in site visitations made by the department internship supervisor and to conduct an evaluation of the intern using the Fitchburg State College Performance Appraisal form. The intern accepts the obligation of confidentiality in the work performed and agrees to familiarize him/her self with and adhere to the organization's relevant policies and procedures, and to the appropriate standards of professional and ethical conduct.

Intern: ______________________ Date: ______________

On-site Supervisor: ______________________ Date: ______________

Dept. Internship Supervisor: ______________________ Date: ______________

APPENDIX 1b.
Sample Completed Internship Agreement

This sample of a completed internship agreement shows how socially constructed learning environments can be stipulated for internship programs. In the description of general responsibilities, it is clear that learning aspects of becoming a member of a practicing community of public relations professionals is an important part of the internship. Moreover, the student's learning objectives support this by identifying that one interest is determining what it means to be a successful professional in her discipline. Based on the description and the intern's objectives, specific tasks and strategies were chosen to foster an environment that would lead to the attainment of those goals, as well as to determine the success of the internship upon its completion.

APPENDIX G
INTERNSHIP AGREEMENT

This agreement is to be completed within the first two weeks of the internship.

Student's Name: ______________________ I.D.#: ______________

Current Address: ______________________ Current Phone#: ______________

Organization's Name: ______________________

Address: ______________________

On-Site Supervisor: ______________________ Title: ______________

Phone#: ______________________ Extension: ______________

Descriptive title of internship: ______________________

Description of general responsibilities and/or activities:

Being well organized, have a desire to be a team player, have solid PC
ills in Microsoft Office & having a knowledge of graphic programs is a plus.
uties include organizing monthly luncheons, research (press releases) & assisting
/ mailings to members, layout & design of monthly newsletter, updating monthly
lendar of events, website inputting & posting, & also answering phone & tradeshow activities.

Statement of learning objectives (what the intern wants to learn):

Want to learn how PR works & runs, willing to learn everything &
ything. Want to learn aspects of PR, (press releases, newsletters & calendars
& events). Want to learn & network w/ people they work w/ & are involved w/
r the business. Want to learn how to be an effective PR employee for a company.

Identification of tasks and strategies (how the intern will attain the objectives):

By listening, observing & taking tasks head-on. Trying my best to
effective & being able to help w/ the load of daily activities. Be willing
go & try things out in the field & then being able to apply them to
mpany expectations. Help in making the company flow. Also, by networking w/ director at company luncheons

Time span on internship (dates): From: 5/24/04 To: 8/27/04

Minimum daily work hours of internship:

Mon. 8 Tues. 8 Wed. 8 Thur. 8 Fri. 8 Sat. ______ Sun. ______

The undersigned have read and agree to all the conditions set forth. Furthermore, the on-site supervisor agrees to provide the intern with an orientation concerning relevant organizational policies, procedures and functions, to manage the intern's work assignments, to meet with the intern regularly, and to be available for counsel and advice during the internship. He/she also agrees to participate in site visitations made by the department internship supervisor and to conduct an evaluation of the intern using the Fitchburg State College Performance Appraisal form. The intern accepts the obligation of confidentiality in the work performed and agrees to familiarize him/her self with and adhere to the organization's relevant policies and procedures, and to the appropriate standards of professional and ethical conduct.

Intern: ______________________ Date: ______________

On-site Supervisor: ______________________ Date: ______________

Dept. Internship Supervisor: ______________________ Date: ______________

APPENDIX 2a. Academic Supervisor's Evaluation Form

The academic supervisor's evaluation form is used to record impressions and evaluations of periodic assignments for each supervisory visit. This becomes the record of the internship. Academic supervisors make a prescribed number of visits to the internship site during a given semester. The purpose is to meet privately with the internship supervisor in order to gain an understanding of the intern's performance to date. Following that meeting, the academic supervisor meets with the intern, pointing out what the intern is doing successfully and identifying areas that need improvement. These sessions can also serve to resolve any uncertainties regarding the academic assignments for the internship.

At the conclusion of the internship, this form is one of the artifacts; the observations recorded in it can be used to help determine the final grade for the experience.

Fitchburg State College
"The Leadership College"

INTERNSHIP VISITATION RECORD

Name: ______________ Fac. Advisor: ______________

Current Address: ______________ Zip: ________ Home Telephone: ______________

I.D. Number: ______________ Internship Organization: ______________

Address: ______________ Zip: ________ Organization's General Telephone: ______________

Intern's Telephone: ______________ Site Supervisor: ______________

Supervisor's Telephone: ______________ Start Date: ________ End Date: ________

I. Visitation Date: ________ Time: ________ Person Contacted: ______________

Location: ______________ Log: ______________

Ss. Work Obs.: ______________

Assignment #1 ______________ Assignment #2 ______________

Assignment #3 ______________ Assignment #4 ______________

Notes: ______________

II. Visitation Date: ________ Time: ________ Person Contacted: ______________

Location: ______________ Log: ______________

Ss. Work Obs.: ______________

Assignment #1 ______________ Assignment #2 ______________

Assignment #3 ______________ Assignment #4 ______________

Assignment #5 ______________ Assignment #6 ______________

Notes: ______________

III. Visitation Date: ________ Time: ________ Person Contacted: ______________

Location: ______________ Log: ______________

Ss. Work Obs.: ______________

Assignment #1 ______________ Assignment #2 ______________

Assignment #3 ______________ Assignment #4 ______________

Assignment #5 ______________ Assignment #6 ______________

Assignment #7 ______________ Assignment #8 ______________

Assignment #9 ______________ Assignment #10 ______________

Notes: ______________

Evaluation Final Grade: ________ Comments: ______________

APPENDIX 2b.
Site Supervisor's Evaluation Form

The site supervisor's evaluation form is used to facilitate an end-of-internship performance review, similar to an annual or semiannual professional performance review. After the form is completed, we ask that the supervisor review it with the intern. Typically, the academic supervisor will again meet first with the site supervisor to review the intern's performance for the duration of the internship. Following that meeting, the academic supervisor will then meet with the intern one final time to review the internship, the intern's strengths, and areas for improvement. The evaluation form provides the basis of this meeting. If necessary, strategies for continued professional growth can be identified and discussed at this time.

APPENDIX E
FITCHBURG STATE COLLEGE PERFORMANCE APPRAISAL

Student Intern: ______________________________ Date: __________

Company, Institution, or Agency: ______________________________

Address: ______________________________

Carefully and fairly evaluate the performance of the student intern in terms of the following qualities	Unacceptable	Needs Improvement	Meets Normal Expectations	Exceeds Normal Expectations	Attains Excellence	Does Not Apply	Comments
1. **Quality of Work:** Consider accuracy, thoroughness, and reliability of result; number of errors; frequency of redoing work; desire to do it right; advocacy of high standards.							
2. **Quantity of Work:** Consider the volume of work produced under normal conditions; speed with which work is done; consistency in keeping up with workload; ability to adjust to and meet quick turnaround demands.							
3. **Creativity:** Consider accomplishments in devising ways and means for doing new jobs; talent for having new ideas; suggestions for new and better ways of doing existing jobs; proclivity for being imaginative.							
4. **Job Knowledge:** Consider the command of knowledge essential to job performance; the understanding of principles, methods and processes to be used; experience, education and specialized training.							
5. **Judgement:** Consider ability to determine proper courses of action; recognition of when to ask questions; appropriateness of decisions; avoidance of impulsivity and indecisiveness; degree of common sense.							
6. **Adaptability:** Consider speed of learning new duties, grasping explanations, willingness to try new concepts and adapt them; ability to work effectively alone or as a team member; disposition to work within existing managerial structure.							
7. **Initiative:** Consider drive to attain goals; demonstration of an active effort to do more; desire to increase responsibilities; indications that the individual is an energetic self-starter; evidence that the individual sees work needing to be done and proceeds appropriately; willingness to proceed alone; propensity to take necessary steps to get things done.							
8. **Time Management:** Consider whether individual usually arrives at work on time; meets schedules and deadlines; establishes priorities; makes efficient use of uncommitted time.							
9. **Attendance:** Consider number of days (whole or part) lost due to illness and/or personal reasons; willingness to work beyond required hours to complete tasks.							
10. **Neatness:** Consider desire to maintain neat, orderly work area; willingness to clean work area after tasks are completed; personal appearance and dress appropriate to position.							
11. **Maturity:** Consider propensity to take assigned tasks (menial and challenging) seriously; accepts criticism graciously; does not bring personal problems to work; willingness to accept consequences of decisions.							
12. **Commitment:** Consider level of genuine commitment to the career field; pride in work; investment of time and energy in becoming more effective and knowledgeable; participation in professional meetings and organizations.							
13. **Communications Skills:** Consider adeptness at oral and written communication; inclination to keep supervisor and colleagues informed; willingness and openness to share information.							
14. **Problem Solving Skills:** Consider ability to handle assignments that are complex and beyond the average; proficiency in analyzing a situation and getting to the point quickly; readiness to identify problems and suggest solutions; thinking at the conceptual level.							
15. **Cooperativeness:** Consider flexibility; willingness to assist others without being asked; ability to get along with peers; possession of a positive, agreeable, and constructive demeanor.							
16. **Reaction to Stress:** Consider dependability when deadline pressures intensify; ability to remain calm and effective despite irritations, change in plans, new plans; evidence of high frustration tolerance.							
17. **Integrity:** Consider the presence of ethical and forthright behavior; commitment to responsible, reliable and trustworthy conduct; willingness to admit mistakes, being honest and truthful in deeds and words; existence of a sense of fair play; actuality of courteous comportment; tendency to meet commitments and obligations.							

Please comment on the following items.

1. If there was an opening for an employee in the area of work this student intern is now performing, would the student intern be a serious contender for the position? ☐ Yes ☐ No

   If no, indicate what action the student intern should take to make himself/herself competitive. ____________

   ____

2. Areas for improvement are:

   a. ____

   b. ____

   and these can be strengthened by doing the following:

   ____

   ____

   ____

   ____

   ____

3. Areas of strength are:

   a. ____

   b. ____

   and these can be further strengthened by doing the following:

   ____

   ____

   ____

   ____

   ____

____

On-Site Supervisor's Signature Date Intern's Signature Date

Signatures indicate form has been discussed by field supervisor with intern.

APPENDIX 2c. Sample Completed Internship Evaluation

This sample of a completed internship evaluation (despite the handwriting) demonstrates the type of specificity that is useful in a performance evaluation of this kind. The rating chart on the first page, shows clearly what the intern has accomplished and what areas need improvement. Even more important are the descriptive comments included on the second page, which provide ample information for discussion at the conclusion of the internship. This evaluation helps the intern, as well as both supervisors identify workable strategies to aid in the transition to full successful employment.

FITCHBURG STATE COLLEGE PERFORMANCE APPRAIS

Student Intern: ______________________ Date: ____________

Company, Institution, or Agency: ______________________

Address: ______________________

Carefully and fairly evaluate the performance of the student intern in terms of the following qualities:

	Unacceptable	Needs Improvement	Meets Normal Expectations	Exceeds Normal Expectations	Attains Excellence	Does Not Apply	Comments
1. *QUALITY OF WORK: Consider accuracy, thoroughness, and reliability of results; number of errors, frequency of redoing work; desire to do it right; advocacy of high standards.*				✓			Intern is a reliable assi[stant,] sets high goals and standards.
2. *QUANTITY OF WORK: Consider the volume of work produced under normal conditions; speed with which work is done; consistency in keeping up with workload; ability to adjust to and meet quick turnaround demands.*				✓			Managed to assist 4 photographers during bus[y] session.
3. *CREATIVITY: Consider accomplishments in devising ways and means for doing new jobs; talent for having new ideas; suggestions for new and better ways of doing existing jobs; proclivity for being imaginative.*		✓					With time and experien[ce] toward end of internshi[p] was less shy to
4. *JOB KNOWLEDGE: Consider the command of knowledge essential to job performance; the understanding of principles, methods and processes to be used; experience, education and specialized training.*				✓			Considering the "studen[t] status" is rea[dy] to enter professional fi[eld]
5. *JUDGEMENT: Consider ability to determine proper courses of action; recognition of when to ask questions; appropriateness of decisions; avoidance of impulsivity and indecisiveness; degree of common sense.*		✓	✓				only area to improve asking questions earlier [to] get proper course of action effect sooner.
6. *ADAPTABILITY: Consider speed of learning new duties, grasping explanations, willingness to try new concepts and adapt them; ability to work effectively alone or as a team member; disposition to work within existing managerial structure.*					✓		Great team player, very mature.
7. *INITIATIVE: Consider drive to attain goals; demonstration of an active effort to do more; desire to increase responsibilities; indications that the individual is an energetic self-starter; evidence that the individual sees work needing to be done and proceeds appropriately; willingness to proceed alone; propensity to take necessary steps to get things done.*					✓		Contributed by produc[ing] 3 to 4 photographs for ed[iting] per day during last [...] of internship (approx. 75 to 100)
8. *TIME MANAGEMENT: Consider whether individual usually arrives at work on time; meets schedules and deadlines; establishes priorities; makes efficient use of unscheduled time.*			✓	✓			Always working. Doesn't need promp[ting]
9. *ATTENDANCE: Consider number of days (whole or part) lost due to illness and/or personal reasons; willingness to work beyond required hours to complete tasks.*					✓		Never missed a da[y]
10. *NEATNESS: Consider desire to maintain neat, orderly work area; willingness to clean work area after tasks are completed; personal appearance and dress appropriate to position.*			✓				Removed trash daily. Cleaned up work a[rea] regularly!
11. *MATURITY: Consider propensity to take assigned tasks (menial and challenging) seriously; accepts criticism graciously, does not bring personal problems to work.*					✓		Very polite and thank[ful] for input. Always up bea[t]
12. *COMMITMENT: Consider level of genuine commitment to the career field; pride in work; investment of time and energy in becoming more effective and knowledgeable; participation in professional meetings and organizations.*					✓		Continued to produce own personal art, go to lectures, exhibits. Wants t[o] network with assistants.
13. *COMMUNICATION SKILLS: Consider adeptness at oral and written communication; inclination to keep supervisor and colleagues informed; willingness and openness to share information.*			✓				[...] outgoing nature is a great asset.
14. *PROBLEM SOLVING SKILLS: Consider ability to handle assignments that are complex and beyond the average; proficiency in analyzing a situation and getting to the point quickly; readiness to identify problems and suggest solutions; thinking at the conceptual level.*			✓				With time intern will excell in this area.
15. *COOPERATIVENESS: Consider flexibility; willingness to assist others without being asked; ability to get along with peers; possession of a positive, agreeable and constructive demeanor.*					✓		[...] is a pleasure to work with.
16. *REACTION TO STRESS: Consider dependability when deadline pressures intensify; ability to remain calm and effective despite irritations; changes in plans, new plans; evidence of high frustration tolerance.*					✓		Consistent level of calm demeanor.

Please comment on the following items.

1. If there was an opening for an employee in the area of work this student intern is now performing, would the student intern be a serious contender for the position? ☑ Yes ☐ No
If so, indicate what action the student intern should take to make himself/herself competitive.

2. Areas for improvement are:
a. Be bolder, more agressive in persuit of information or express
b. Of opinion 2) Listen to instructions and if you don't agree express it, if you don't agree and don't express it, follow The instructions.

and these can be strengthened by doing the following:

It is hard to change a person's demeanor, especially when part of it is cultural But be aware That This area of improvement, (being more agressive) is also strength, because he has tremendous patience— Just find a balance That works.

3. Areas of strength are:
a. Great talent for photography
b. willingness to learn.

and these can be further strengthened by doing the following:

Keep photographing, printing, See exhibits. Work with as many commercial studios as possible. Develop a price structure for your work, or else you will be taken advantage of. Keep in touch with everbody at

On-Site Supervisor's Signature Date Intern's Signature Date

Signatures indicate form has been discussed by field supervisor with intern

APPENDIX 3.
Internship Liability Form

On occasion, some organizations will request a formal liability waiver before agreeing to host an intern. This form has been useful for documenting the waiver. Any academic department would, of course, expect to work closely with the college or university legal counsel in developing such a form. And when the form is required by an internship host site, it is always a good idea to meet with the intern and explain what the form means in terms of protection and responsibility.

APPENDIX F
SAMPLE LIABILITY RELEASE

In consideration of (name of organization) permitting (name of intern-name of college) to visit its facilities at (address of organization) for the purpose of an internship on (dates), (name of intern-name of college) hereby agrees to defend, idemnify and hold (name of organization) and its affiliates, harmless from any and all claims or losses resulting from personal injuries, including death, resulting therefrom and/or damage to the property of (name of intern - name of college), its agents, servants, invitees, students, teachers, or to third parties, as a result of the use of the premises by (name of intern-name of college) and/or any of the foregoing persons during such visits to (name of organization) facilities and occurring in or upon such facilities. This idemnification shall include all reasonable costs, expenses, and liabilities incurred in connection with any such injury, loss or damage or any such claim or any proceedings brought thereon or in defense thereof.

Furthermore, if it becomes necessary for (name of organization) to disclose proprietary and confidential information to (name of intern-name of college), it is understood that (name of intern-name of college) will not disclose said proprietary and confidential information unless released in writing by (name of organization).

Finally, (name of intern-name of college) will make full and prompt disclosure to (name of organization) of all inventions, improvements, discoveries, developments, and ideas, whether patentable or copyrightable or not, made or conceived by (name of intern - name of college) in connection with or as a result of said internship. If (name of organization) should decide that it is not interested in exploiting said items, (name of organization) may decide to release said items to (name of intern - name of college) outright or grant (name of intern - name of college) such lesser rights as it may decide.

Signature of intern: ______________________ Date: ______________

Approved by:

Education Institution

Name of Institution: ______________________

Name of Official: ______________________

Title: ______________________ Date: ______________

Host Organization:

Name of Organization: ______________________

Name of Official: ______________________

Title: ______________________ Date: ______________

APPENDIX 4a.
Daily Log Form

This particular Daily Log form provides one of several options for students in recording their daily activities. It is perhaps the most minimalist approach to recording important documentation of the internship's daily activities. For that reason, in addition to providing the form, we also encourage students to design their own form, as long as it communicates the information contained in this one.

We hope to see interns adopt methods of daily documentation that also include their reflections on what they have been asked to do, how well they were prepared to do it, how successful they were, and general impressions regarding how their daily tasks inform them of the professional and cultural milieu of their chosen discipline. We seek to have the internship develop reflective thinkers, as well as doers.

Internship : Daily Log

Date:__________ Mo Tu We Th Fr Sa Su

Left House: ______ Arrived: ______ Left :______ Arrived Home:______ Total CommuteHours: ☐ Total Work Hours: ☐

Tasks Performed	TIME	Facts/ Concepts Learned

People to Remember (Name, Title, Co., Address, Fax/Phone #)	Three weekly accomplishments (To be completed Friday pm)

Additional Thoughts

APPENDIX 4b.
Sample Completed Daily Log

In this sample, one can notice a variety of things. First, the student chose to redesign the form so that it met her needs. But beyond that, the impressions recorded are limited to the cryptic documentation of what was done on a daily basis. We would have preferred to know more about the intern's thinking while she was doing these tasks and her perception of how the tasks related to the learning objectives she had previously identified. As a result, while this completed form meets minimal expectations for documenting the internship, it does not provide access to the intern's thoughts and reflections about her experience and how it prepares her for a career in this profession.

*** This list includes most of the major tasks that I performed during my time at BJ's Wholesale Club. However, more inconsequential tasks (eg: photocopying documents) are not listed, but were often part of my daily routine.***

Tuesday June 1, 2004

- Research Shell and Mobil Annual Reports
- Begin compiling Clip Report
- Team meeting
- Individual meetings with S. Bebas, A. Russ, and N. Sodano

Wednesday June 2, 2004

- Continue with Clip Report
- Begin researching communities for grand openings
- Scanned newspapers for articles/topics for Journal (trends, etc)

Thursday June 3, 2004

- Continue with Clip Report
- Continue with grand opening research

Friday June 4, 2004

- Day off

Monday June 7, 2004

- Continue with grand opening research
- Made calls to various newspapers/radio stations about press release
- Timed Holiday '03 broadcast tapes
- Continue with clip report

Tuesday June 8, 2004

- Begin daily google news search on home heating oil
- Sorted credit card related files
- Began editing/reformatting donations rejection postcard
- Checked publication for BJ's mention
- Researched gas articles in local papers

Wednesday June 10, 2004

- Sorted, organized and alphabetized credit card related files

APPENDIX 4c. Student Journal

The following selections from a student journal represent a particularly good example of documenting an internship, combining a record of the activities the intern participated in, his accomplishments, and his reflections regarding internship experiences. These selections clearly indicate the type of thinking we advocate for an intern. Not only does the intern describe in detail the responsibilities he was given, he records his impressions of the internship site's culture, the professional approaches the internship supervisor adopts with regard to his work, and even the intern's thoughts about living in a new environment and the challenges that entails.

Thursday June 4th, 2004

Today was the first day of my internship at PM Studios in NYC. I started out by arriving at work ready to do a photo shoot with Peter Jennings one of the two photographers there, the other being Max Shuppert. I have been very excited to start my internship, I see it as a stepping stone to the next level, a leap to my professional career, whatever that may really be. The shoot was with Aerosoles, just some catalogue shots for them with plain white backgrounds. They were repeating clients who Peter knew well so the atmosphere was relaxed. Danielle the studio manager who will be a prevalent character in my life at the studio was there helping out. Max wasn't around since it was Peter's shoot. Peter does all products and Max tends to do more fashion type work. They have known each other for some time, I got their history from Alabama to Dallas, to New York. The shot was quick and smooth. I am going to have to get accustomed to the free meals provided by the company wanting the shoot done.

Peter is very liberal with the way he communicates, swearing up a storm all over the place. His mannerisms are familiar to that of people from the Boston area, where he is originally from. He is a likeable person who says what's on his mind, we get along well through our similar styles of humor. He is a bit more crass and I guess you could say politically incorrect than myself but that doesn't bother me any. Max took the day off, so I suppose I wont work with him until tomorrow.

After the shoot Danielle (Dani) showed me around the studio space which is spacious and beautiful. It is pretty much what I dreamt as the perfect studio space in NYC. The ceilings are around 20 feet high, the doors and furniture are modernistic and polished metal. There are high tech goodies lying all around and equipment of the best quality. They all use Macs and the camera set up is primarily a Mamiya 645 with a PhaseOne digital set up. It is powerful and fantastic. Although next week Peter says he will be bringing in his Sinnar 4x5 for a shoot for Tylenol I believe. The studio is great and I am contemplating in my mind what I can do all summer during the downtimes to keep busy. There is a promise of reorganizing and cataloguing the entire studio's inventory! This despite ht grunt work of the task sounds fantastically exciting, proving my photo-geekdom.

My place of living is working out well, I am renting a room from a friends sister in Astoria Queens for $300 a month plus utilities. It is a small room with access to the rest of the small house. It is spacious enough and living with people I know is much better. I like where I am for the time being and that is important.

Friday June 5th, 2004

Friday was a shorter day, I met Max for the first time. He is a quiet (compared to Peter) intelligent man, who I get along with well. I talked with him about his background and how he came to be where he is now. We talked about the things we were going to do during the internship, and such. Later Danielle showed me how to apply for a street photography permit when shooting on location in Manhattan. You have to go through quite the rig amoral faxing papers back and forth so you wont get a fine when shooting on the street. It's only limited to people who want to set up tripods and block areas of streets and such, it doesn't really pertain to just randomly going around shooting.

In the afternoon we went out for lunch and then it was decided we would come in and start fresh on Monday. The schedule of photo shoots was outlined and then I went on my way. I went down to Canal St. and found the tattoo shop my friends work at and then later met up with a bunch of my friends who I know from here and we went out to dinner. Good times had by all.

Monday June 7th, 2004

I spent most of my morning first watching Peter retouch his pictures in photo shop so he can print a book of work specifically shot on white backgrounds, otherwise known as silhouetting. I watched him for a few hours as we talked, we get along well. Before lunch he told me it was my turn, so he had me 'dust' a lot of the images, so I went through and got rid of digital dust and small imperfections on the products, it was fun. I probably will learn more in the first week of photo shop work with Peter Jennings than I learned in all of my years at Fitchburg. Later I went through the studio and cleaned, sweeping the floors with the big dry mop, a task I will be doing regularly. There is fortunately very little grunt work, the bathrooms are all operated by the building itself so I don't have to worry about those, the only other big thing is taking the trash out, which is not hard, I can assure you.

Max spent most of his day devising his new promo books, I had helped him design a layout the day before and now he had finalized the plan. They will be about 2 inches by 3 _ inches big and have about six pages total. He finally decided on printing them double sided and use a ribbon like object to tie them together instead of glue. We did a few glue tests and since I will be an implemented tool in putting the 95 books together that he wants to do it is easier to tie one ribbon than glue 600 pages. He is sending the books out to a list of potential clients and then after a few days when he thinks they have them he will call them and offer his services. Business is slower in the summer and the opportunity for promoting yourself becomes more of the daily task rather than the task itself. Peter told me that it is harder to actually get the work than it is to do it. Once you have a good repertoire of skill sand are confident lighting things in just about any situation your only real obstacle is getting jobs.

Tuesday June 8th, 2004

Today was the first photo shoot with Max. He was doing a favor for a make up artist friend of his (Josh) by doing a fashion layout for his friend Tim who is trying to become a professional model. Max told me he prefers shooting women but the job is there, although to him very unexciting. Tim showed up with a small entourage and a mini Pomeranian dog. He was very high fashion, one of the so called 'fabulous' people that Max likes to shoot, although the stuff he usually does is far more true high fashion, Tim was more of a wanna be I suppose. I had a great time setting up 6 different lighting situations with Max and watching him work. I am truly surprised he doesn't have a steady clientele of big name people coming through, he is a very nice guy and knows how to tell when a model knows how to actually model. Today was exciting and exhausting and the start of what seems to be great photo shoots with both the photographers I am interning with, I am pleased with where I am right now.

Wednesday June 9th, 2004

Peter decided we needed to go out to Chelsea so he could look t portfolio books for his new silhouette book of work. The key here seems to be if a client asks you if you have a body of work to show in a certain subject, make a professional looking book of work to show them or they will just pass you right by. We visited about 3 shops and finally decided to get some nice leather cover floppy books. A smaller one for his new book and a matching larger one for his old portfolio, he wants to reprint it and put it in the new book. We ate lunch out and then headed back to the studio where we did an impromptu shoot for the design company that shares our floor. It was more work than its worth for me I suppose since I was the one setting up all the lights and taking them all down so Peter could hit the shutter about 5 times. It was about 45 minutes of work for me just to do it all. I'm not complaining though, just pointing out its not always good to be the unpaid intern. I wish I was a paid assistant in times like that.

The rest of my day was spent cutting and folding Max's new promo books which are looking very cool. Dani bought a few ribbon samples and we tied up a few books. By the end of the day we had 18 of them finished. It takes quite awhile to print them all out and wait for the paper to dry enough so we can cut and fold them. I have become an efficient well oiled machine. I like this kind of creative work, it is inspiring. I want to make my own now!

Thursday June 10th, 2004

This morning Peter and I went over to the B and H store. It is the biggest camera store I have ever scene in my life, they have everything, it was awesome. I also took my first taxi ride in Manhattan on the way there. We got back and I learned a few more handy photo shop tools as Peter was finishing the printing on his silhouette book. Then the next and better part of the day was spent putting together Peter's new book, I put all the photo corners in the pages, measuring carefully so it would look just right. In the end it turned out really good. I am learning a whole lot about making books digitally and they sure are nice looking. This is by far a modern studio where Digital is the medium of choice, everything gets scanned anyway, I learned the design group next door has a drum scanner too! Next Max's girl friend showed up and help him start a series of stock photography of people, an idea he has to make a small portfolio of work to show average everyday people in a pro studio lit kind of set up instead of the fabulous people all the time. A new angle, he keeps the ideas flowing even in the time of less clients, very motivating. I then got the keys to the studio as Peter will be taking a long weekend since tomorrow is his birthday. I have to be there around 9ish so that if the package with the film comes before Max gets their I can load the 4x5 film for the Tylenol job next Tuesday so we can do tests on Monday. I have to go rent the equipment we need on Monday as well, or rather pick it up. I'm glad they trust me enough to do this so early on!

Friday June 11th, 2004

Went in early to intercept a package of film that we need for the shoot on Tuesday, I had to load some film holders for the test shoot on Monday morning. I went to Alkit for the first time, one of the photo stores they rent equipment from on a regular basis to drop off some equipment that Danielle used on Thursday night. Today was slow and only Max came in, so I cut and folded what he had printed out for his promo books and then he sent me home when he went to a lunch date that he intended not to return from. Got some good work done even though I was only there a little while.

APPENDIX 5a. Instructions for Daily Log Summary

At the conclusion of their internships, students in the Department of Communications Media internship program at Fitchburg State College are responsible for completing and submitting two assignments that become part of the official record of their internship. One of these is the Daily Log summary. In it, students are asked to list the activities and responsibilities they were assigned, along with what they learned from each.

Completing this assignment requires interns to reflect on their experiences and to project how those experiences provide a foundation for future professional growth. Even in situations where they have learned that they do not want to pursue the field professionally, thinking through the process that brought them to that conclusion is a vital aspect of learning—about a profession and about themselves. This document is used to orient future potential interns to the particular internship site recorded in the summary.

Instructions for Internship Daily Log Summary

Create a typed report, which can be in the form of a two-column list, listing the various tasks you performed during your internship and describing what was learned. This information should be summarized from your log. It will be important for you to reflect upon the entirety of your experiences, focusing not only upon what you learned that can be perceived as being directly related to your professional preparation, but also upon what you have learned about yourself and your fit into your chosen profession.

APPENDIX 5b.
Sample Daily Log Summary

The following sample Daily Log summary is an excellent illustration of a student achieving the goals of this assignment. Not only does she identify the specifics of what she did and what she learned, but she includes important reflections on what she learned, particularly her own professional growth in knowledge and confidence.

VARIOUS TASKS	WHAT WAS LEARNED
I had a lot of Photoshop assignments, such as fixing the unfixed photographs for the sections of 8 Days a Week, News and Features, and Arts.	Files and folders were stored in the BPEdit server. For each section of the paper there were various numbers of photographs that either had to be color-corrected or converted into black and white. Each photograph had to be set to its proper tones. I also learned that each photograph is different and should be treated as such. After the photograph was corrected, it had to be determined which section it belonged to. I gained much more knowledge and confidence with Photoshop and also got use to what looked right in a photograph as opposed to what just looked ok.
I scanned photos, negatives, chromes, and slides.	Got very familiar with the two scanners in the office. With each photograph comes a different way it should be scanned in. Sometimes it is at 200 resolution at 100 percent, others, like slides, it is better to scan it in at 200 resolution at 150 percent.
I downloaded images from the Nikon Digital coolpix4300.	Taking the Digital camera out for most of my assignments I had to download the images I shot from the camera to the computer. Then took the necessary steps of saving and correcting the image before placing it into the specific folder.

Tear-Sheets, when one, such as the internship, goes through each paper and takes out photographs and illustrations so that they can be sent to the artist for his/her portfolio.	Other than the photographers and illustrators that freelance for the company, everyone gets their work sent to them. Thus comes in the interns who work on the Tear-Sheets. I like the idea that the company does it because it sends out the message that they do appreciate one who summits work. Even though this was the "keep you busy work" they gave me, it was interesting to see others work.
Filing the photographs in the filing cabinets.	I learned that all filing is, is an organizational job. There are several different subsections to the photo files. They are: music, film, people, subject, sports, tv, theater, classical, dance and art. Needless to say, I got lost sometimes, and other times I was not.
I was sent out on assignments to take various photographs for articles usually in the sections of Hot Plate, On the Cheap, Sipping and/or Noshing (which can be found in the 8 Days a Week). I also had work submitted in the DNC special section paper and had an ad photograph in Stuff and Night Magazine.	When I would first get an assignment I would have to search on www.mapquest.com to get directions to the specific restaurant or bar, then I had to call them and set up a time that was good for me to go in and shoot. Calling and talking to different places got me to be professional and tasteful on the phone. Each assignment was a different learning experience. Getting into the photography field I learned what type of photograph would be suitable for certain occasions. I learned various ways of making a photograph work for not only my own view of it, but also other people's as well.

APPENDIX 6a.
Instructions for Final Paper

The other major assignment for which interns are responsible at the conclusion of their internship is the final paper. Essentially an analysis report, this paper provides insight to the history, stability, and culture of the internship site. It also provides interns with an opportunity to reflect upon their experiences while on internship.

In order to provide a modicum of consistency across our internship program, we specify the types of research we would like interns to perform in analyzing their site. We want them to develop abilities in assessing professional organizations that they can use later when exploring potential employment. With these abilities, prospective employees can determine whether or not an employer's environment is conducive to their professional growth and success, how well they are qualified for entry into that employer's business and culture, and the likelihood that they could achieve the kind of considered excellence Aristotle identifies as the hallmark of a successful person.

Instructions for Final Internship Paper

Prepare a typed term paper profiling the company organization with which you are interning. The purposes of this paper are for you to understand that there is some important information you need **before** you agree to work for a group, and for you to learn how to research an organization. Such knowledge is critical to a successful job hunting campaign.

In profiling your company, be sure to provide the following information:

a. The history of the company and of the department you are interning with. Include a look at the economic (for example, is it publicly or privately owned?), geographic (for example, was it always in the same location?), and organizational (for example, what was the growth of the organizational hierarchy?) past.

b. The economic outlook (expansion or downsizing plans for employees, space, equipment, budgets, clientele, products/services, departments, profits) of the company/department.

c. The type of product/service provided by the company and your department.

d. The marketing strategy of the company and of your department.

e. The salary range of an entry-level communicator in your department as well as the range of fringe benefits that could be expected for both a freelance/contract and full-time employee.

f. The corporate culture of the company and department. What are the accepted rules and norms (often unspoken and informal) about how you should behave in the organization? Examine such things as the work ethic, social norms, dress codes, political climate, avenues for conflict resolution, language when speaking (formal or informal English) congeniality of relationships, levels of bureaucracy, degree of closeness, and channels/types (formal or informal) of communication, acceptable humor, and scheduled versus normal work hours.

g. The advantages and disadvantages of being a communicator in the type of company you are interning with.

APPENDIX 6b.
Sample Student Final Paper

The following sample student final paper shows an intern meeting the requirements for the final analysis paper. She has researched her internship site fully, reports on the results of that research, and includes her own considered opinions regarding the site and her experience there.

Internship Paper

Eduventures, Inc. is a research and consulting firm dedicated to supporting the growth of organizations operating in the Pre-K-12, Higher Education and Corporate Learning markets. Eduventures was founded in 1993 in order to fill a void in the education market. Since then, the company has produced, created, and developed the first industry research of its kind along with an online resource for news and analysis. Eduventures has also developed an annual subscription model for providing broad-based industry support to hundred of key clients. Eduventures is privately held in Boston, Massachusetts where their home base is located at 20 Park Plaza, Suite 1300.

Eduventures, Inc. serves leading organizations and provides them with the analysis and insight to education businesses, technology vendors, financial firms, educational institutions, and other firms with large stakes in the market. Some of their key clients include: Accenture, McGraw-Hill, Collegis, DeVry, PeopleSoft, and Sylvan Learning Systems.

In order for the company to maintain their successful relationships with key clients, the department of marketing and event management is responsible for planning conferences and communicating with members of the media so that they can increase Eduventures visibility as well as show that they are the leading authority on the education industry.

Another department found in the company is Client Services, which ensures a high-level of satisfaction to clients as well as provides them with the service and support they need.

The Research and Advisory sector of the company produces the main product of the firm. They are responsible for providing customized and proprietary client deliverables for subscribers to Eduventures research services. The subscribers can receive reports and white papers that are produced by the research group on current issues and trends in the education industry. The research group also writes quarterly newsletters and alerts on breaking news across the educational spectrum.

As for their product and services, they offer clients an annualized, renewable relationship that produces measurable business results. Its research package includes: access to all of the company's research products, quarterly updates and strategy sessions, one-on-one briefings following all report releases and market positioning and business development support.

The final two departments found in the company have to do with hiring/firing and the budget. The Human Resources department deals with the management of hiring, firing, orientation, benefits, retention, personal relations, communication and corporate culture for the employees. On the other end, the finance department manages accounts payable along with creating monthly financial reports for the Board of Directors. This department also supports business development activities by providing team members with background materials on new companies.

This year Eduventures has branched out to form the Learning Collaborative, which focuses on E-Learning. Executive Vice President, Peter Stokes along with Vice President of Marketing, Brent Keltner are working together to review and forecast the performance of competing for-profit E-learning universities, for-profit spin-offs of traditional universities, and technology firms that are providing the software and services necessary to support outsourced E-learning solutions. They are also attempting to improve services, enhance recruitment learning, and generate new revenues through E-learning. The two hope to find what successes, failures, trends and strategies lay beyond this type of learning method.

Besides Eduventures' research services, the advisory services offer a supplement to the research package so that they can provide a more customized and proprietary client deliverable. The type of projects the advisory practice works on is evaluating new market opportunities, producing custom primary and secondary research, providing growth strategy development and conducting customer surveys and analysis.

Not only is Eduventures widely recognized for their research and advisory services, but are most noted for hosting world-class trade shows and exhibitions. These events address the needs of the Corporate, Higher Education and Pre-K-12 buying community. That of course is only one way Eduventures markets their services. Another way the company markets their services is by sending out welcome cover letters to would-be clients who have a relationship with top players in the education industry. And since the company is the authority on the education market, an additional way they get exposure is by having their data and analysis cited by leading news and information sources. These include: Wall Street Journal, New York Times, Newsweek, Education Week and the Chronicle of Higher

Education. When reports are produced, these leading news sources receive a copy before anyone else does on Eduventures' press list, which includes a broader and more varied range of education publications.

As for Eduventures corporate culture, the core staff is a compilation of unique and talented individuals who share a high energy and an ability to work independently as well as in a team, deadline driven environment. The staff also conducts themselves in a professional, considerate and mature manner. They exhibit strong and analytical skills and interpersonal skills which make Eduventures seem even more attractive to their consumers. Dress code is subjected to business casual and work hours consist of a nine to eleven hour work day. As for the internship experience as a whole, I think Eduventures was a great place to work. I got to see how a company of this size functioned as a whole and how they functioned within their departments. I think as a whole, Eduventures' staff needs to work on their communication. From what I saw, it seemed as though there was a lack of communication or sometimes even confusion when it came time to communicate with other staff concerning project deadlines or report deadlines. It seemed as though certain people didn't always adhere to their deadlines and instead tried to please others by contradicting themselves and saying that they would get their work done, but instead put it on the back burner.

Another thing that I noticed to be a little strange was, when I attended the marketing meetings, Lisa, who is the Marketing Manager at Eduventures always led the meetings. From my viewpoint, I would think that the Vice President of Marketing would lead the agenda and make sure that things are getting done according to schedule.

On the other hand, working for such a small company allowed me to see those types of things that I probably wouldn't see if I was working for a larger company. I think working here definitely shed some light into the kind of organization I want to work for. One thing that was good about my Eduventures experience was getting to work with and form a close relationship with my mentor, Liz Roessler as well as forming other bonds with other EV staff members that I have collaborated with during my time here. I think the Eduventures Associate Program has been a great learning experience which has helped me get involved and has taught me a great deal. I will definitely take what I've learned here and apply it to my job in the real world.

APPENDIX 7.
Student Résumés

While there are numerous designs that students might adopt in creating a résumé for internship placement, the following examples demonstrate a range of design options, each of which permits students to display their abilities to their fullest. Samples have been chosen to illustrate a number of methods by which students can design the interplay of text and white space in order to strategically present their qualifications. Of particular interest are the designs that permit a considerable amount of important information to be included, make that information accessible, and still maintain the one-page limit common to entry-level employees and interns.

APPENDIX 7a.
Student Résumé—Graphic Design

Objective	To obtain an internship in the field of Graphic Design that will build upon my design skills and generate the experience needed to become an advanced designer and illustrator.
Education	B.S. Degree in Communication Media with a concentration in Graphic Design as well as a minor in Art. Fitchburg State College, Fitchburg, MA Year of Graduation: Spring 2004.
Academic Profile	Layout & Design; Human Communication; Graphic Arts Production; Graphic Management; Graphic Design Photography; Typography; Media Criticism; Pre-press production; Computer Graphic Design; Art Appreciation; Communication Law and Ethics; Water Based Media; Advanced Painting; 19th Century Art
Related Skills	Working knowledge of Adobe Photoshop, Adobe Illustrator, QuarkXPress, and familiar with InDesign.
Work experience	May 2000 – Jan. 2003 Hoyts Cinema Corporation. Boston, MA **Box Office Representative** Responsibilities included verifying as well as correcting theatre information such as ticket grosses and concession sales. Also filed as well as received and distributed theatre information to other Box Office Representatives. Jan 1998 – Aug 1998 Washington Park Market. Boston, MA **Night Crew Stock Clerk** Responsibilities included supplying shelves with groceries and maintaining the store in a customer friendly appearance overnight for the morning shoppers. Summer 1997 Bain & Company. Boston, MA **P.C. Repair Department Internship** Responsibilities included assisting the repair dept. with hard drive updates as well as swaps. Performed memory upgrades to older P.C.'s as well as conducted inventory of laptops.
Honors	Dean's List Spring 2002, Fall 2002, and Spring 2003.

References and Portfolio available upon request.

APPENDIX 7b.
Student Résumé—Film/Video Production

OBJECTIVE

To obtain an internship in film and video post-production working on music videos, commercials, film or television production.

EDUCATION

B.S. in Communications/Media with a concentration in Film and Video. To graduate from Fitchburg State College in Dec. 2001.

ACADEMIC PROFILE

- Advanced Film Production
- Advanced Digital Production
- Post Production
- Advanced Editing Techniques
- Macintosh Technical Training
- Sound Design
- Multimedia Tools & Techniques
- Human Communications Technology
- History of Film
- Lighting for Film & Video
- Communications Law & Ethics
- Scriptwriting

PRODUCTION EXPERIENCE

Editor / Sound Design - Responsible for recording audio during production and the post-production. Post-production duties include digitizing and syncing all footage, cutting the film, post-production audio, titles, and compositing. Also responsible for the graphic design of all press materials.

- *Plot Fever*, 2000. 16mm dark comedy short – "Who says greed is a sin? In the world of cemetery plot real estate, one man engulfs a community. Behold the rise and fall of Lester Combes."
- *Commerce*, 2001. 16mm experimental short – "Journey through beautiful snows covered landscapes with two young travelers."
- *Driving Charlie*, (also Co-Writer) 2000. 16mm comedy short – "Welcome to Ace's Ultimate Driving Academy - You are about to embark on the most worthwhile experience of your life... so buckle up!"
- *Discovery.com Spoof*, 2000. 16mm comedy short – "Have you heard of the website Discovery.com? Sasquatch and friends parody these original ads."

SOFTWARE

- AVID MCXpress
- AVID Media Composer
- AVID Film Composer
- Apple Final Cut Pro
- Media 100 LE
- Digidesign Pro Tools
- Adobe After Effects
- Adobe Photoshop
- Macromedia Director
- Pinnacle Commotion Pro
- AutoCAD

EQUIPMENT

- Movieola 6 plate flatbed
- Nagra 4.2
- Sennheiser MKH416T
- CP 16mm Camera
- Canon X-L1 MiniDV Camera
- Sony VX-2000 MiniDV Camera
- Sony TRV-900 MiniDV Camera
- omni & lavalier mics
- Sony MiniDisk MZ-R55

HONORS

- *Plot Fever* featured in:
  - Cinequest 2001 Film Festival (rated one of the 10 best film festivals in the world by the *Ultimate Film Festival Survival Guide*.)
  - Durango 2001 Film Festival
  - First Glance Philadelphia 2001
  - John Hopkins 2001 Film Festival
  - Valleyfest 20011 (Ran a nationwide commercial with clips from Plot Fever. Featured on the Independent Film Channel, March 2001.)
  - Contrast 2000 Film Festival.
- *Driving Charlie* featured:
  - in the Visions 2000 Film Festival
  - on www.studentfilms.com and was the highest rated and most watched film for two months December 2000 and January 2001.
- Creative/Management Committee for 2000 Contrast FSC Film Festival, and for 2001 Visions FSC Film Festival.
- Deans List 5 semesters
- Winner of the Rhode Island Youth AutoCAD Architectural Design Competition 1997.

INTERESTS

Computers, Skate Videos, Survivor, Basketball, Troubleshooting, and Fresh Air.

APPENDIX 7c.
Student Résumé—Photography

Objective

To acquire an internship through which I can build upon the skills I have achieved in the past four years, as well as to prepare myself for a career in the field of photography.

Education

B.S in Communications/Media, concentration in photography, to be graduated from Fitchburg State College in May 2003.

Academic Profile

- 35mm Photography
- Digital Photography
- Color Photography
- Medium Format Photography
- Large Format Photography
- History of Photography
- Multimedia Tools & Techniques
- Introduction to Graphic Design
- Communication Law & Ethics
- Interactive Media
- Human Communications
- History of Architecture

Related Experience

- Architectural photographer for Living with Antiques magazine
- Wedding photographer
- Advertising shoot for the Piercing Emporium
- Unofficial photographer for Worcester Flower Show, 2001
- Volunteer photographer for Habitat for Humanity, 1999
- Sears portrait photographer 1999

Related Skills

Working knowledge of Adobe Photoshop, Macromedia Flash. Familiar with Director 8.5, Cinema 4d XL7

Proficient with medium format cameras from:

Hasselblad, Mamiya, Bronica and Fuji

Experience with strobe lighting kits by,

White Lightening, Novatron and Speedotron

Working knowledge of large format cameras using Zone System exposure and development techniques.

Honors

Work exhibited in Visions 2000, 2001, and 2002

Architectural work on cover of Living with Antiques September 2002

Dean's List Spring 2001

APPENDIX 7d.
Student Résumé—Professional Communication

Objective	To obtain an internship in the field of public relations that will utilize and build upon my writing, organization, and communication skills in order to prepare myself for a career in public relations and promotion.
Education	B.S. in Communications/Media with a concentration in technical writing. Fitchburg State College, Fitchburg MA GPA 3.65 Year of graduation: Spring 2003
Academic Profile	Public Relations Marketing Advertising Copywriting for Advertising Feature and Magazine Writing Technical Documentation Media Writing Writing for Business and Technology Human Communication Interpersonal Communication Communications Law and Ethics Multimedia Project Design Financial Accounting Cultural Anthropology
Related Experience	*Writer:* *The Point* (school newspaper) *Public Relations and Promotions*: Researched and coordinated a public relations and promotions campaign for the Newman Center, the on campus Catholic Church.
Related Skills	Proficient with Microsoft Word; familiar with Adobe FrameMaker and Excel.
Work Experience	Waitress, Applebees Bar and Grill 2001-present Waitress/Trainer, Weathervane Seafood Company 2000-2001 Office Assistant/Customer Service, YMCA 1999-2000
Honors	Dean's List every semester
Interests	Horseback riding, field hockey, weight and cardiovascular training, skiing, poetry, painting
References	Available upon request

APPENDIX 8.
Sample Student Personal Statement

Increasingly, we are asking students to include in their portfolio a personal statement that describes who they are and their aspirations—not only for internship but for their professional careers, as well. The purpose of these statements, again, is to foster reflective thinking on the part of the prospective intern, so that they enter their internship with mature expectations, recognizing their strengths and weaknesses, their wants and desires, and how internship might best serve each of these. Thinking in such ways while preparing for the internship goes a long way toward establishing valuable patterns of thought that will guide interns as they reflect on their experiences during their internship.

Career Statement

I consider myself a creative thinker with a variety of talents and interests. First among these interests is research information and looking at the gathered materials from many different perspectives. I also enjoy the creative work in marketing by promoting businesses in innovative ways. I am interested in taking a step back and analyzing the different types of interpersonal relationships working within each situation, business, or market I am studying. I find myself having the best ideas and creative aspirations when I am working with clients. It brings me great pleasure to help a person and/or business grow by showing them how to introduce themselves in fresh new ways through the many marketing styles. My portfolio encompasses the kinds of work that I take pleasure in the most, and have been most inventive. It shows my way of concisely thinking through new ways to present material, whether it is a research proposal, an advertising campaign, or otherwise and I feel it will be a strong asset to help me enter the field of marketing and promotions.

Description of Relaxation by Design Advertising Campaign

This portion is the major part of an advertising campaign for a client-individualized day spa I developed called *Relaxation by Design.* It includes a situation analysis, brochure, grand opening flyer, discount postcard, and a business card which are all important pieces in building a business from the ground up, and targeting a specific type of audience. In this case the target audience is businessmen and women in the Boston area, as well as nearby college students.

Description of Danielle Miraglia Public Relations Campaign

The following are the components of a public relations campaign for a local singer/songwriter with goals of trying to get her name out to a larger audience and developing a tour along the East Coast. I created a campaign plan, personal letter to radio stations, and a pitch letter and feature story for a local newspaper that she uses to help promote herself and her Fall release date of her CD, "Nothing Romantic."

Description of Codependency in Intimate Interpersonal Relationships

I developed this research proposal due to an interest in analyzing the different kinds of relationships people have and hoping to solve issues that may arise. I took on this challenge to educate people about codependent relationships, because not many people are even aware of the issue at hand. My goal was to help people recognize and change the codependent way of thinking in intimate interpersonal relationships.

APPENDIX 9.
Sample Portfolio Entry

The following sample entry illustrates the design method we have adopted for most student portfolios. The two-page spread is adapted from the modular design common to some technical manuals. On the left-hand page of a two-page spread, the summary describes the contents and purpose of the portfolio entry. The actual entry appears on the right-hand page of the same spread. If the entry is a multiple-page document, a sample page would be selected, with the complete document located at the end of the portfolio.

Typically, we ask students to prepare portfolios with a range of 8 to 12 entries that demonstrate a variety of proficiencies within their discipline. Professional writers, for example, might include samples from such persuasive discourse as press releases, public-service announcements, and campaign reports; or from such analytical discourse as technical manuals and project conclusion reports. Graphic designers might include samples of print graphics, screen captures of motion graphics (or if the portfolio is presented in electronic form, the motion graphic itself), illustrations, corporate branding, and so forth. For every discipline, students, in consultation with their advisors, should be able to develop portfolios that support their knowledge and skills.

Sony® Vaio™ PS/2 Wheel Mouse

General Description

The Sony® Vaio™ PS/2 Wheel Mouse is the standard pointing device included with the Sony® Digital Studio™ series of personal computers. The mouse features two buttons. The left button is normally used to interact with the objects on the screen, and the right is used to bring up special menus. These functions can be changed by the user. There is also a scroll wheel that allows for simplified scrolling in some applications.[1] The mouse connects to the computer tower with a PS/2 type of pin connector.

Specifications

Device type	Standard pointing device
Buttons	3 (including integrated scroll wheel)
Interface	PS/2 compliant mouse port
Cord length	4 feet
Current	25mA
Voltage	5.5V

Operational Description

There is a rubber ball inside the mouse that maintains contact with the surface on which the mouse is placed. As the mouse moves, this contact causes the ball to move as well. The ball also maintains contact with two roller bars inside the mouse. Movement of the ball causes the roller bars to spin. One bar reacts to horizontal motion of the mouse, while the other reacts vertical.

[1] See documentation of individual applications for compatibility and special instructions.

(This sample does not hold true to the normal design.)

Writing Portfolio

This mechanical description was prepared as an academic assignment for a writing class. The purpose of the assignment was to explain a device with moving parts. The description should be comprehensive, logical, and easy to understand.

Because the exact functioning of a mouse is complicated and largely carried out by the computer's operating system, I found it useful to limit my description to the mechanical features that send information to the computer. The process of interpolation by the computer is mentioned in context, but I did not attempt to describe the exact methods of the programming.

Index